Psalm 91

Psalm 91

God's Protection Policy

Paul Brewster

SUNESIS MINISTRIES LTD

Psalm 91: God's Protection Policy

Copyright © 2016 Paul Brewster. The right of Paul Brewster to be identified as author of this work has been asserted by him in accordance with the Copyright, Designs, and Patents Act 1988. All rights reserved. No part of this publication may be reproduced or transmitted in any form or by any means, electronic or mechanical, including photocopy, recording, or any information storage and retrieval system, without permission in writing from the author.

ISBN 978-0-9935147-0-8

Published by Sunesis Ministries Ltd. For more information about Sunesis Ministries Ltd, please visit:

www.stuartpattico.com

Unless otherwise indicated, Bible quotations are from the Holy Bible, King James Version.

Where indicated: Scripture quotations taken from the Amplified Bible, Copyright © 1954, 1958, 1962, 1964, 1965, 1987 by The Lockman Foundation. Used by permission. (www.Lockman.org)

The author of this book does not dispense medical advice or prescribe the use of any technique as a form of treatment for physical, emotional, or medical problems without the advice of a physician, either directly or indirectly. The intent of the author is only to offer information of a general nature to help you in your quest for emotional and spiritual well-being. In the event you use any of the information in this book for yourself, the author and publisher assume no responsibility for your actions.

The views expressed in this book are solely those of the author and do not necessarily reflect the views of the publisher, and the publisher hereby disclaims any responsibility for them.

I dedicate this book to my beautiful wife Lorraine who has been a tremendous help and support throughout our years of marriage. Love you.

Contents

Introduction	9
Faith: God's Assurance Policy	12
The Secret of His Presence	22
Our Twofold Deliverance	31
The Shield of Truth	40
Freedom From the Spirit of Fear	50
In the World but not of this World	59
The Holy Spirit: our Habitation and Refuge	69
Jesus Christ: our Passover Lamb	82
The Protective Ministry of Angels	95
The Dominion of the Believer	106
The Sevenfold Will of God	118
Persecution in the Light of God's Protection Policy	130
Bibliography	143

Introduction

Since the fall of our forbears into sin, humanity has been plagued by wickedness and natural disasters such as sickness and diseases, earthquakes and floods, famines, wars and conflicts, whirlwinds, tornados, tsunamis and so on. These calamities are bent on plunging humanity into ultimate demise and extinction. But for the grace and love of God, Jesus exclaimed, when he gave His prophetic discourse, on the Mount of Olives, concerning the end time signs of His coming, "And unless those days were shortened, no flesh would be saved, but for the elect's sake those days will be shortened" (Matt. 24:22 NKJV).

These temporal evils are so intertwined in the cycle of life and society that many take out a variety of insurance policies to protect themselves in the event of suffering some adverse calamity. There are all kinds of insurance you can sign up to: accident insurance, life insurance, property insurance, and the list goes on. However, these insurances do not actually protect you from the things for which you are insured, nor do they stop those events from occurring. Their protection is only of a monetary nature to prevent making further payments that would impact on finances during the aftermath.

But in the plan of redemption, there is a protection policy that far exceeds any policy that men could make, a divine policy that guarantees absolute protection even in the midst of tragedy and trouble, so that your life is unaffected by what is occurring around you because you are covered by the Presence of the All-Powerful God. And in this, writes the psalmist: "Thou shalt hide them in the secret of thy presence from the pride of man: thou shalt keep them secretly in thy pavilion from the strife of tongues" (Ps. 31:20 KJV)

Divine protection is God's promise today for His people as it was in biblical times. We are currently living in perilous times, predicted by the Apostle Paul (2 Tim. 3:1). Jesus prophesied in Matthew 24 that there would be an increase in frequency and intensity of deception, wars, famine, pestilence, earthquakes and defines them as the beginning of birth pangs (Matt. 24:8).

As these prophetic signs intensify, God's people must know how to appropriate their inheritance of protection from every evil that is coming on the earth to try men. God has provided a divine shelter and covering that will separate the righteous from the unrighteous, and in this, the world will see that the God of our Lord Jesus Christ is the true and living God (Jn. 17:3).

God has outlined our protection policy in Psalm 91 and this is the purpose for God instructing me to write this book, so that His people can know and walk in their inheritance of protection purchased by the blood of Jesus Christ. May your eyes be opened to His wisdom.

1

Faith: God's Assurance Policy

"Now faith is the substance of things hoped for, the evidence of things not seen" (Heb. 11:1).

Insurance is defined by the Collins Dictionary as "...the act, system, or business of providing financial protection against specified contingencies, such as death, loss, or damage... the state of having such protection... Also called insurance policy, the policy providing such protection..." In this definition, the only protection insurance policies provide is financial, and even then, it is not an absolute guarantee because of unforeseen anomalies. Human organisations and companies are limited to what they can do and are dependent on the fluctuation of the stock market. It is not possible for men to grant us absolute protection. And to this agrees the words of Jesus:

"...With men it is impossible, but not with God: for with God all things are possible" (Mk. 10:27 KJV).

God's plan of protection for the believer is not an insurance policy but an assurance policy because it guarantees absolute protection, for the Bible says in Numbers 23:19 (KJV), "God is not a man that he should lie; neither the son of man that he should repent: hath he said, and shall he not do it? Or hath he spoken, and shall he not make it good?

Although God is all-powerful and has made provision for your protection in these last days, it will not come to you automatically; will have to appropriate it. A rich man may give a cheque of one million pounds to a poor man but if he doesn't bank the cheque, he will remain poor even though he is legally rich. In the same vein, God has legally provided protection in the atonement of Jesus Christ but unless you appropriate it you will be subject to the same calamities as the people who do not know God. The way you appropriate your inheritance of protection is by faith. Faith is the means by which you receive anything in the Kingdom of God. Faith is our assurance policy, meaning that we already have whatever we have asked for. The opening scripture of this chapter states:

"Faith is the substance of things hoped for, the evidence of things not seen" Heb. 11:1 KJV).

The Amplified Bible says it in this manner:

"Now Faith is the assurance (the confirmation, the title deed) of the things [we] hope for, being the proof of things [we] do not see *and* the conviction of their reality [faith perceiving as real fact what is not revealed to the senses].

Faith is the DNA of the righteous, for the Bible exclaims,"...The just shall live by faith (Rom. 1:17 KJV). And if you are righteous, you are pleasing God, for without faith, it is impossible to please God and by it the elders obtained a good testimony that they were righteous (Heb. 11:2, 6). To every born again Christian, God has dealt the measure of faith (Rom. 12:3). Faith's DNA is inherent in the Believer and so it is our responsibility, as Christians, to understand and use it. DNA is defined according to the Collins Dictionary as, "A substance present in nearly all living organisms as the carrier of genetic information and is responsible for the transmission of hereditary characteristics.

This definition of the natural is a reflection of true spiritual realities; so faith's DNA can be defined like this: a spiritual substance present in all righteous organisms and is responsible for the transmission of divine characteristics (see 2 Peter 1:4; 1 Jn. 3:9). Faith's genetic information and transmission of hereditary and divine characteristics emanates from the Word of God for the Scripture states,

"...faith cometh by hearing and hearing by the word of God" (Rom. 10:17 KJV). And "Being born again, not of corruptible seed, but of incorruptible, by the word of God, which liveth and abideth for ever (1 Peter 1:23 KJV).

Because of being born of the Word, the Bible goes on to declare, "...as he is, so are we in this world (1 Jn. 4:17c KJV). As we are like Him on the inside, let us work it out on the outside by constantly and consistently feeding on the Word of God (see 1 Peter 2:2).

Faith's DNA is an acronym that represents the following three essential aspects to the nature of faith:

1. D is Definition of faith
2. N is Necessity of faith
3. A is Application of faith

DEFINITION OF FAITH

"Now faith is the substance of things hoped for, the evidence of things not seen" (Heb. 11:1 KJV).

There is no better definition of faith than what is described in the above scripture. Faith has two elements: substance and evidence. The term "substance" is from the Greek word "hupostasis" and it refers to the substance and reality of something, the basic essence, the existence and actuality of a thing. Since faith cannot be seen or perceived by the physical senses (2 Cor. 5:7), it is spiritual, invisible substances or realities that can be perceived only by the human spirit. The Apostle Paul confirms it this way: "We having the same spirit of faith according as it is written..." (2 Cor. 4:13 KJV). Therefore, faith is the response of the human spirit to the Word of God (Oyakhilome 2005).

Faith is spiritual substance; it is the reality and existence of things which are hoped for - expectation of things which are not seen (Rom. 8:24-25). This statement means that when you pray in faith about a promise or need, you already have the answer to that prayer before it is manifested to your physical senses. That is why Jesus said,

"Therefore I say to you, whatever things you ask when you pray, believe that you receive them, and you shall have them" (Mk. 11:24 NKJV).

The clause: "...shall have them" is preceded by "...believe that you receive them". God's answer comes in two forms: the faith or invisible form, and the manifested or visible form.

When we pray, Jesus exhorts us to receive by faith what we have asked for, and we will see it manifest. Religious prayers merely ask, but faith-based prayers receive (1 Jn. 5:14-15). Your faith is the title deed, like a written document that legally confirms ownership of property. A person who has a title deed to a house does not need to bring his fellow employees to his house to prove he owns a house debt-free; all he needs to show them is his title deed. Actually, without the title deed, there would be no concrete proof that he owns a house even if his colleagues saw him use his key to enter the house; that does not prove it is his house. He could be a tenant paying rent to live there. What he tells his friends and what they see, could be a lie.

In the same vein, whatever we see that is contrary to God's Word, is a lie; the only true reality or substance is faith in God's Word, the title deed of what we already possess in the realm of the spirit. You may be experiencing symptoms of sickness in your body while believing God for your healing but your faith – the title deed – says, "by his stripes ye were healed" (1 Peter 2:24 KJV). Stand on that word and you will see your healing come to pass.

Faith is also the evidence of things we do not see. In other words, it is the proof or conviction of unseen realities. It is the assurance and confirmation of what we already have, but do not see with the physical eye. Therefore faith becomes the eye of the human spirit to see what we already possess in the unseen realm. The Bible states,

"While we look not at the things which are seen, but at the things which are not seen, for the things which are seen are temporal; but the things which are not seen are eternal" (2 Cor. 4:18 KJV).

NECESSITY OF FAITH

"But without faith it is impossible to please him: for he that cometh to God must believe that he is, and that he is a rewarder of them that diligently seek him" (Heb. 11:6 KJV).

If you want to please God, it is only going to be by faith; it is a necessity, an unavoidable condition or prerequisite to pleasing God. The passage of Scripture above is saying that it is impossible to please God without faith. Note, that the phrase 'impossible to please Him' is not preceded by the words, 'without prayer or fasting', 'without giving tithes and offerings', 'without going to church', or 'without preaching or teaching the Word'. You can do all these things and still not please God (Matt. 6:5, 7, 16-18, 1-4; 23:23; 1 Cor. 13:3; Phil. 1:15-16; Rom. 2:19-23).

In the next clause of the verse, it tells us,

"...he that cometh to God must believe that he is, and that he is the rewarder of them that diligently seek him" (ibid.).

Doing all these religious acts of piety must be corresponding actions of faith; they must be spiritual fruits borne out of the root of faith or else they are dead works (Heb. 6:1; 9:14). Works without faith are dead and faith without works is also dead (James 2:14-26). The balance of the Christian life is that true faith will produce corresponding actions that are in harmony with God's Word. Faith will produce obedience but unbelief will produce disobedience (Heb. 11:8; Rom. 16:26; Heb. 3-4). Develop a righteous-consciousness of faith in Christ finished work of redemption, and good works will be the spontaneous result.

Application of Faith

"And Jesus answering saith unto them, Have faith in God. For verily I say unto you, That whosoever shall say unto this mountain, Be thou removed, and be thou cast into the sea; and shall not doubt in his heart, but shall believe that those things which he saith shall come to pass; He shall have whatsoever he saith. Therefore I say unto you, What things soever ye desire, when ye pray, believe that ye receive them, and ye shall have them" (Mk. 11:22-24 KJV).

Prior to Jesus giving His discourse on faith in the above Scripture, a situation had arisen where He was hungry, and saw a fig tree with leaves, expecting it to have fruit. But seeing no fruit on the tree, He cursed the fig tree by saying, "...No man eat fruit of thee hereafter for ever..." (Mk. 11:14 KJV). Then He left the fig tree and went to the Temple. The next morning, as they passed by, Peter called Jesus' attention to the fact that the fig tree He cursed was withered (v20-21). It was from this point that Jesus began to teach His disciples about faith and how to apply it to their circumstances. Jesus commenced by saying, "Have faith in God" or in the Greek text: "Have the faith of God", the key to walking in intimacy with God. It was by this same faith that the Bible stated that Enoch walked with God (Gen. 5:22-24) and had a testimony, by faith, that he pleased Him (Heb. 11:5). It is from this basis of relationship that Jesus teaches His disciples how to apply their faith; first showing them by example - cursing the fig tree, and then teaching them the principle to release their faith. In principle, Jesus taught them to release their faith by speaking to the mountain as He spoke to the fig tree. Matthew's parallel account in his gospel presents the comparison:

"...Verily I say unto you, if ye have faith, and doubt not, ye shall not only do this which is done to the fig tree, but also if ye shall say unto this mountain, Be thou removed, and be thou cast into the sea; it shall be done" (Matt. 21:21 KJV).

Jesus was stating if His disciples would have faith and not doubt in their hearts, they could curse the fig tree as He did and also speak to the mountain to move in to the sea. This truth was not only for the twelve disciples; it is also for His disciples today. We can do the same things that Jesus did, if only we would believe and apply our faith to believe the impossible is possible (Mk. 9:23). Jesus' life and ministry are examples of how we are to live our lives in the faith and power of the Holy Spirit. If we are to do this, we must learn to believe and speak, for this is the spirit of faith,

"We having the same spirit of faith, according as it is written, I believed, and therefore have I spoken; we also believe, and therefore speak" (2 Cor. 4:13 KJV).

Believing with the heart and speaking with the mouth are the two hinges that swing the door of faith open to total salvation (Rom. 10:8-10). These are the principles that Jesus taught His disciples – to believe in God (Mk. 11:22), speak to the mountain and see it removed (v23). This promise is to anyone who will believe it for God is not a respecter of persons but He is a respecter of faith. Jesus prefaced verse 23 with "whosoever":

"...Whosoever shall say unto this mountain, be thou removed, and be thou cast into the sea; and shall not doubt in his heart, but shall believe that those things which he saith shall come to pass; he shall have whatsoever he saith" (Mk. 11:23 KJV).

Jesus mentions "believing" once, but "speaking" three times. It is not enough to believe; you have got to say what you believe. Then in the next verse, He talks about believing that you receive when you pray (v24).

There is a relationship between verse 23, speaking to your mountain, and verse 24 – believing that you receive. It is from a position of believing you receive when you pray, that you speak to your mountain to be removed, whether it is sickness, depression, financial debt, demons or death in your life or someone else's. You speak with authority commanding the problem to go in Jesus Name. We do not talk to God about the problem; we speak to the problem about God.

This principle is beautifully depicted in the ministry of Jesus who commanded sickness and disease to leave; demons to come out and people to be raised to life again (Matt. 8). In the raising of Lazarus from the dead, Jesus' mindset was that He believed He received when He prayed saying,

""..Father, I thank thee that thou hast heard me. And I knew that thou hearest me always: but because of the people which stand by I said it, that they may believe that thou hast sent me. And when he thus had spoken, he cried with a loud voice, Lazarus come forth. And he that was dead came forth..." (Jn. 11:41b-44a).

This is a vivid example of Jesus releasing faith and power through speaking. Let us learn to only confess God's Word and refuse to succumb to doubt and unbelief in negative circumstances that are contrary to divine truth. The Bible says that life and death are in the power of the tongue (Prov. 18:21). Only say what God says, is the meaning of the Greek word for "confession" (homologeo), to speak the same thing." Confession is used in two ways: to build your faith (Josh. 1:8) and to release your faith (Mk. 11:23).

It was important to cover the subject of faith so that you know how to appropriate the benefits of God's protection, because faith is the assurance and confirmation of what is promised to us, and is already ours in His Word (Heb.11:1 Amp.). Now let us begin to delve into Psalms 91: our Protection Policy.

2

The Secret of His Presence

"He that dwelleth in the secret place of the most High shall abide under the shadow of the Almighty. I will say of the LORD, He is my refuge and my fortress: my God; in him will I trust" (Ps. 91:1-2).

The benefits of protection in Psalm 91 are comprehensive, covering every spiritual and temporal evil known to mankind. Bible scholars believe this psalm was authored by Moses because it follows Psalm 90 which is entitled "A Prayer of Moses the man of God". Both begin with the same subject matter: the dwelling place of God. Psalm 90:1 (KJV) states,

"LORD, thou hast been our dwelling place in all generations".

And Psalm 91:1:

"He that dwelleth in the secret place of the most High shall abide under the shadow of the Almighty.

Before talking about the blessings, we must come to know and follow after the Blesser; the divine Protector and Deliverer. This is the purpose of the Christian life. The place to which the children of Israel were heading after their deliverance from the bondage of Egypt, was Mount Sinai; not the Promised Land. They needed to meet the Promiser prior to entering the Promised Land of Canaan, or else they could not have conquered the nations of the land and would have succumbed to the idolatrous practices.

The purpose in bringing them to Mount Sinai is seen in the words spoken by God to Moses in Exodus 19:3-4 (KJV),

"And Moses went up unto God, and the LORD called unto him out of the mountain, saying, thus shalt thou say to the house of Jacob, and tell the children of Israel; Ye have seen what I did unto the Egyptians, how I bare you on eagles' wings, and brought you unto myself".

All the miracles and signs of the ten plagues that God performed in Egypt; the pillar of cloud by day and the pillar of fire by night; the supernatural provisions of manna, quails and water gushing forth from the rock were a means to a greater end – to meet with God,

"And Moses brought forth the people out of the camp to meet with God; and they stood at the nether part of the mount" (Ex. 19:17 KJV).

Through the miraculous signs that God did for His people, He carried them on eagles' wings but in meeting them at Mount Sinai, He desired them to come under the shadow of His wings: the place of perpetual fellowship in His Presence, but they drew back to stand afar off because they did not have the fear of the Lord to draw near (Ex. 20:18-21; Deut. 5:23-30). The children of Israel drew back from God's presence that was meant to be their divine protection for their journey and destination ahead. But the Israelites failed because of disobedience and unbelief (Heb. 3-4).

God is our Dwelling Place (Ps. 90:1), and He is inviting us to dwell and live in His Presence: the secret place of the most High (Ps. 91:1). The place of fellowship and intimacy in His Presence is the secret place,

"Thou shalt hide them in the secret of thy presence from the pride of man: thou shalt keep them secretly in thy pavilion from the strife of tongues" (Ps. 31:20 KJV).

The secret place is the secret of His Presence where the believer is kept and preserved and delivered from the plots of the enemy and the strife of tongues. This reminds me of the passage of Scripture which proclaims,

"No weapon that is formed against thee shall prosper; and every tongue that shall rise against thee in judgment thou shalt condemn. This is the heritage of the servants of the LORD, and their righteousness is of me, saith the LORD" (Is. 54:17).

This secret place is where you are supposed to dwell, and the word "dwelleth" is from the Hebrew term: "yashab" meaning to sit, remain and dwell. The verb carries the sense of ascending a throne (1 Kings 1:46); to sit on anything; to remain, stay or linger; to dwell; to dwell in a house, city or territory. By virtue of these definitions, we can live and remain in that secret place twenty four hours a day because it is our home, our habitation or dwelling place. God is our dwelling place provided for all generations (Ps. 90:1) because it is where He has purposed for us to continually abide. God's secret place is the place we ascend to sit as on a throne.

Since Psalm 91 has its fulfilment in Christ – in fact all the promises of God are fulfilled in Christ (2 Cor. 1:20) – the New Testament declares:

""Even when we were dead in sins, hath quickened us together with Christ, (by grace ye are saved;) And hath raised us up together, and made us sit together in heavenly places in Christ Jesus" (Eph. 2:5-6 KJV).

Each of us has our particular heavenly place in Jesus Christ to which we have ascended, where we are to rule and reign in life (Rom. 5:17). The secret place is our position of authority with Christ in the heavenly realm; that is why it is called the secret place of the Most High. The Most High is the highest authority in the universe. The Hebrew rendering is "elyon" which refers to the highest; something that is high or higher; the uppermost; and it is derived from the Hebrew root: "ala" meaning to go up, to climb or ascend. Elyon is used as a reflection of God's exaltedness, omnipotence, majesty and supremacy.

To dwell in that secret place, you must yield your human

authority to the highest authority; when you do so, He delegates His authority to you to use for His Kingdom business. Submission to God's authority will serve to protect you (James 4:7). The word "secret place" is translated from the Hebrew term: "seter" and it refers to a hiding place derived form the Hebrew root: "satar" meaning to hide or conceal, hence the notion of protection. God's biblical principle of submission to authority was designed to bless and protect; not curse or destroy. When you come out from under God's authority, you also come out from under His protection.

The second clause of Psalm 91:1 says, "...shall abide under the shadow of the Almighty" KJV). Now concerning the word "shadow," it is translated from the Hebrew term: "sel" (derived from the Hebrew root: "salal"), which means "to be or grow dark." The Hebrew word "sel" communicates the ideas of shade, defence and protection. It is a shade that gives relief from the heat of the sun (Ps. 121:5); a place of protection under the shadow of one's roof (Gen. 19:8).

The Almighty is the shade of protection (Ps. 91:1; 121:5) from the heat of the sun as it was when His Presence appeared as a pillar of cloud by day to shield Israel from the heat of the desert sun during their wilderness journeys (Ex. 13:21-22). God's Presence is able to literally protect you from sun stroke when there is no natural means of defence (Ps. 121:5-6). Also, where there is natural truth, there also exists its spiritual counterpart; fellowship in His Presence will give you relief and refreshing from the heat of afflictions, distresses and persecutions of life (Mk. 4:5-6, 16-17; Acts. 3:19).

The phrase, "shadow of the Almighty" contains the name by

which He will be to His people who abide under His shadow. God's name: "Almighty" is translated from the Hebrew rendering: "shaddai." God manifested Himself as El Shaddai to the patriarchs, especially to Abraham (Gen. 17:1; 35:11; 43:14; 48:3). The rabbinic interpretation of this name is that it is a compound word composed of *she,* "who" and *day,* "enough," and so, Shaddai defines Him as the self-sufficient or all-sufficient One; the bountiful One – the God who abounds in all things – the abundant One. This was the name by which the Abrahamic Covenant was sanctioned because it was a covenant of increase, prosperity and abundant blessings for God said to Abraham,

"That in blessing I will bless thee, and in multiplying I will multiply thy seed as the stars of heaven, and as the sand which is upon the sea shore; and thy seed shall possess the gate of his enemies; And in thy seed shall all the nations of the earth be blessed; because thou hast obeyed my voice" (Gen. 22:17-18).

God's covenant of increase included spiritual and temporal blessings. Wealth, in biblical times, was not merely measured in silver and gold but in increased posterity and land, which is what God promised to Abraham (Gen. 12:1-3; 13:14-17) including all the spiritual blessings in Christ – the Seed of Abraham (Gal. 3:12-14, 29).

Here is presented two main aspects to abiding in the secret of His Presence designated by God's Names: Elyon (most High) and Shaddai (Almighty). The former represents authority and the latter, abundant blessings. In that secret place, God will bestow upon His people authority and abounding blessings as also conveyed in Psalm 16:11 (KJV).

"...in thy presence is fullness of joy; at thy right hand there are pleasures for evermore."

Both aspects of the secret place – the Presence of God - are also presented in the above verse. The right hand of His Presence represents authority and Jesus Christ fulfilled this Messianic passage when He was raised from the dead and ascended to sit at the right hand of God, exalted to be the head over all things (Mk. 14:62; 16:19; Eph. 1:20-21; Col. 2:10). The second aspect: "...there are pleasures for evermore" refer to abundant blessings that every believer ought to enjoy under the shadow of the Almighty: the All-Sufficient One.

These two aspects are revealed in the New Testament. Firstly, I have mentioned before that every believer in Christ has been raised up with Him, and made to sit in heavenly places in Christ – our position of authority (see Eph. 1:20-22; 2:5-6) Secondly, we have not only been raised to an authoritative position but also to enjoy all spiritual blessings from that position as God's Word states,

"Blessed be the God and Father of our Lord Jesus Christ, who hath blessed us with all spiritual blessings in heavenly places in Christ" (Eph. 1:3 KJV).

These blessings are only fulfilled as we abide in Christ (2 Cor. 5:17; Jn. 15) and walk in the Spirit (Gal. 5:16). In Christ, you are to live by faith in the finished work of Calvary and walk in the power of the Holy Spirit, that is why it is vitally important that every believer is baptised with the Holy Spirit evidenced by speaking in tongues for He is the manifested Presence of God (Ps. 139:7; Lk. 1:35; Acts 1:8; 2:1-4).

In the outset of Psalm 91:2, it tells us that the person who dwells in that secret place will have the right confession:

"I will say of the LORD, He is my refuge and my fortress: my God; in him will I trust" (Ps. 91:2 KJV).

And at the end of the verse, it declares that the confession is a confession of faith. Our talking must be in harmony with God's Word, saying what God has already said – from which we get the Greek meaning of the word "confession," *homologeo: to speak the same thing.* The psalmist's personal confession is that God is his refuge and fortress. In the Hebrew language, the word for refuge is "mahseh", signifying a place of shelter, derived from the Hebrew root: "hasa" - to seek refuge, flee for protection, and figuratively, to put one's trust in God. He is our refuge in the storms of life (Ps. 14:6; 46:1; 62:7; 94:22). A refuge, a place of shelter, is a strong and formidable place of protection; this is who God is to every one that puts their trust in Him.

Fortress is from the Hebrew word "metsuda;" it is a military stronghold from where a soldier fights to defend or attack an opposing army. With the Lord as our fortress, we have been commissioned by the LORD of hosts (the armies) to fight the good fight of faith, promising to keep and protect us while engaged in battle. The Apostle Paul exhorts us to stay in our fortress as we engage in spiritual warfare:

"...be strong in the Lord and in the power of his might" (Eph. 6:10 KJV).

Having God as our fortress equips us to be strong in Him and not in ourselves since we are no match for the archenemy. As long as we fight from our divine Fortress, God, we will overcome every strategy that the devil brings against us. God is our Fortress in times of battle.

Lastly, the psalmist confesses the Lord to be his God. The name "God" is translated from the Hebrew rendering: "Elohim" that describes the Lord as being strong. It is derived from the Hebrew root "El", meaning strong One. The Lord is looking to see who will put their trust in Him so that He can show Himself strong. That strength is not something that remains on the outside. The Lord comes to dwell on the inside of His people to impart His strength to them. The Bible states,

"..the people that do know their God shall be strong, and do exploits" (Dan. 11:32b KJV).

3

Our Twofold Deliverance

"Surely he shall deliver thee from the snare of the fowler, and from the noisome pestilence. He shall cover thee with his feathers, and under his wings shall thou trust: ...." (Ps. 91:3-4 KJV).

First of all, the striking feature in the above verses is that they present the Lord God of Israel and His faithful people under the metaphor and imagery of a fowl or bird. In verse 3, the believer is said to be delivered from the snare or trap set by a hunter of birds, called a fowler; then, verse 4 describes the living God to have feathers and wings. Obviously, these are not literal descriptions of God and His people but only serve to convey some important spiritual truth concerning God's providential care and protection over His people.

These metaphorical descriptions of God and His people can be seen in other passages of Scripture. For example, when God delivered Israel from Egypt and brought them through the wilderness to Mount Sinai, He said,

"Ye have seen what I did unto the Egyptians, and how I bare you on eagles' wings, and brought you unto myself" (Ex. 19:4 KJV).

Eagles' wings expresses God's tender loving care and providential leading towards His people to bring them to Himself. Moses recounts Israel's wilderness wanderings, in another passage of Scripture, using the same imagery:

"As an eagle stirreth up her nest, fluttereth over her young, spreadeth abroad her wings, taketh them, beareth them on her wings: So the LORD alone did lead him..." (Deut. 32:11-12a KJV).

As the eagle stirs up her nest, God also stirred up Israel to come out of her comfort zone, Egypt, and as an eagle flutters her wings over her young, the Lord fluttered His wings to teach Israel how to fly above their circumstances, to develop, mature, and be strong as His people. He took them and carried them on His wings; He carried and sustained them in His care and love (Is. 63:9). As God's children, we are compared to eagles who mount up with wings and utilise the power of flight when the Lord strengthens us:

"But they that wait upon the LORD shall renew their strength; they shall mount up with wings as eagles; they shall run, and not be weary; and they shall walk, and not faint" (Is. 40:31 KJV).

Now, I want to explain the promise of our twofold deliverance in the following passage of Scripture:

"Surely he shall deliver thee from the snare of the fowler, and from the noisome pestilence" (Ps. 91:3 KJV).

This verse begins with "surely", that is to say, the promise of this twofold deliverance is certain. It encapsulates both spiritual and temporal deliverance. They entail the whole salvation package bought and paid for in the atonement of Jesus Christ according to Isaiah 53. The Lord delivers us from the snare of the fowler. According to the Hebrew language, the word for snare is "pah", meaning "a bird trap". It is used in Hosea 5:1 and Amos 3:5, and often refers to calamities and plots: devising to bring about evil, calamity, destruction and harm by which the potential victim is unaware of the consequences and dangers. Birds that fell into traps were unaware that they were traps and that an attractive piece of food was put there to entice and lure them into the trap. Therefore temptation, enticement and deception are central to the function of a snare.

Satan, the archenemy, has set traps for every believer to fall into and he will tempt us with his cunning tricks of deception to lure us into them. These traps are his enticements to sins and offences. But God has made provision for our deliverance from offences. The Bible states,

"[Jesus] was delivered for our offences, and was raised for our justification" (Rom. 4:25 KJV).

Jesus died for our offences and was raised for our justification. Spiritual deliverance is part of our inheritance provided for in the sacrificial death and resurrection of Jesus Christ that makes a soul free and keeps him free (Jn. 8:31-32; Gal. 5:1).

There is a Greek word translated "offence" that conveys graphically the promise of deliverance from the snare of the fowler, and it is the word "skandalon," which was the original name for part of the trap to which the bait was attached. Hence, the "skandalon" was designated for the trap or snare itself. In the New Testament, the term is used metaphorically for an enticement to sin or take some wrong course of action that results in adverse consequences. The word was used of Satan, who through Peter, laid a snare to entice Jesus not to go to the Cross to fulfil God's Will (Matt. 16:22-23); also mentioned of Balaam's teaching that caused Israel to sin (Rev. 2:14); spoken of Christ who is an offence to the disobedient, that by their rejection of Him, they ensnare themselves for judgment of hell (Rom. 9:33; 1 Peter 2:8; 1 Cor. 1:23); and anything that hinders or causes a person to fall (Luke 17:1-2; Mk. 9:42-48). Guard against being offended and becoming the offender by endeavouring to walk in love:

"He that loveth his brother abideth in the light, and there is no occasion of stumbling [Gk skandalon: offence] in him (1 Jn. 2:10).

This verse is the foundational key to walking in freedom from all spiritual bondages and hindrances of the devil.

Temporal Deliverance

"Surely he shall deliver thee from...the noisome pestilence" (Ps.

91:3).

As God's desire is to deliver and preserve us from spiritual evils such as sin, wickedness, anxieties, fears, demonic possession, and the eternal fires of Hell, He has also made provision for deliverance from temporal evil: sickness and disease, plagues, accidents, famine, poverty, violent attacks perpetrated by humans or animals and so on; all these are comprehensively covered in Psalm 91, so that according to verse 16, we can be satisfied with long life. Before explaining verse 3 any further, let us explore the Hebrew definitions for "noisome pestilence". "Noisome" is translated from the Hebrew word "hawwa", meaning "calamity, wickedness, evil desire". It describes the nature of the pestilence – its lust and craving or mischievous desire or evil intent. "Pestilence", translated from the Hebrew term "deber", signifies pestilence, animal disease and plague. This noun is mentioned, in the Old Testament, adjacent to famine, evil, blood, judgment, sword and evil beast. In the book of Jeremiah, the prophetic predictions of divine judgment connects famine, pestilence and sword (14:12; 21:7, 9; 23:10; 27:8). God promises to save us from these evils including sickness, disease and pain, borne and carried away by the substitutionary death of Christ. In the monumental passage of Isaiah 53:4-5, Jesus of Nazareth bore our spiritual evils – sins and iniquities – but also carried our temporal evils – sicknesses, diseases and pains on the Cross:

"Surely he hath borne our griefs, and carried our sorrows: yet we did esteem him stricken, smitten of God, and afflicted. But he was wounded for our transgression, he was bruised for our iniquities: the chastisement of our peace was upon him; and with his stripes we are healed."

The words "griefs" and "sorrows" in the Hebrew language refer to "choliy", meaning sicknesses and diseases, and "makob", meaning pains. So the passage should read,

"Surely he hath borne our [sicknesses, diseases] and carried our [pains]..."

And the passage concludes by saying, "..with his stripes we are healed." Jesus bore our sicknesses, diseases and pains in the same way it says He bore our sins and iniquities (see v5, 6, 11, 12). In the New Testament, Matthew quotes the Hebrew sense of verse 4 when applying the fulfilment of it to Jesus healing the demon-possessed and the physically sick, saying,

"When the even was come, they brought unto him many that were possessed with devils: and he cast out the spirits with his word, and healed all that were sick: That it might be fulfilled which was spoken by Esaias the prophet, saying, Himself took our infirmities and bare our sicknesses" (Matt. 8:16-17).

Matthew's commentary from his Gospel confirms that Jesus took our physical infirmities and sicknesses in His sufferings and death on the Cross. It is for this reason that the Apostle Peter writes, "...by those stripes ye were healed" (1 Peter 2:24c), thus using past tense verbs to stipulate that your healing is a done deal – an established law in the realm of the Spirit. Jesus has borne and carried our sicknesses, diseases, infirmities and pains in the same way that He took our sins upon Himself. The word "borne" is translated from the Hebrew term "nasa", which literally means to lift, bear, carry away or take away. Its Hebrew synonym "cabal", conveys the same idea. This notion graphically sets forth a picture of one lifting and taking a burden of another upon himself and bearing or carrying it away so that the person whose burden it was might be free of it. That is what Jesus did for us; He took upon Himself our sicknesses and diseases and carried them away so that we might be free of them. His body was wounded, bruised and broken for our healing; therefore "...with His [wounds] we are healed" (Is. 53:5). There is no need for God's children to put up with sickness, diseases and pains because Jesus took them upon Himself and bore them away.

God's Will is that His people walk in divine health because it is provided in the blood covenant of Jesus. God's promise of healing and health to Israel in the old covenant is also true for every believer in Christ today. When Israel came out of Egypt and journeyed in the wilderness to arrive at Marah, God declared His covenant of healing to His people saying,

"And said, if thou wilt diligently hearken to the voice of the LORD thy God, and wilt do that which is right in his sight, and wilt give ear to his commandments, and keep all his statutes, I will put none of these diseases upon thee, which I have brought upon the Egyptians: for I am the LORD that healeth thee" (Ex. 15:26).

In this promise of healing and health, God sanctions His promise with His redemptive name: Yahweh-Ropheka that is translated in this verse, "I am the LORD that healeth thee" (ibid.), also meaning the LORD thy Physician. The promise of healing is attached to the name of God, forming a compound name. Yahweh is the redemptive name that is derived from the Hebrew verb: "eheyeh, "to be." It was by this that God made Himself known to Moses as the "I AM" (Ex.3:14).

God's Name refers to Him as the self- existent One, whose existence did not originate from anyone or anything; His life is self-sustaining. Additionally, because God's character, nature and life did not originate in time but existed in eternity, this makes Him immutable and unchanging in His being. Therefore, God's promise of healing annexed to His Name as Yahweh-Ropheka affirms it is always God's will, desire and character to heal. It is not the case that He sometimes does not desire to heal, for that would be inconsistent with His redemptive Name and character.

In the New Testament, the same Yahweh-Ropheka became flesh, dwelt among us and was given the name Jesus; He went about doing good and healing all who were oppressed of the Devil (Acts. 10:38). There was never an instance in the Gospels where Jesus refused to heal a sick person who came to Him. He revealed the unchanging nature of Yahweh-Ropheka in His public ministry. And today, the Bible states,

"Jesus Christ the same yesterday, and to day, and for ever" (Heb. 13:8).

Jesu Christ being the same yesterday, today and forever is tantamount to calling Him Yahweh-Ropheka. The extent to which God forgave us our sins is the degree to which He has healed us of our diseases according to Psalm 103:3:

"Who forgiveth all thine iniquities; who healeth all thy diseases"

This shows that God's attitude towards sins is the same towards diseases, for Jesus bore them both away – our spiritual sins and our physical diseases.

Our Twofold Deliverance

4

The Shield of Truth

"...his truth shall be thy shield and buckler" (Ps. 91:4c)

Truth presented in the opening verse is referred to as God's Truth; whatever He thinks, perceives, understands or agrees with, is truth. It is the quality of being true, real and factual as opposed to what is false. God is declared, in Scripture, to be a God of truth (Deut. 32:4).

There are two aspects of divine truth: the essence or Person of truth, and the contents and principles of truth expressed in words. The former is supported by Jesus Christ when He said to His disciples,

"...I am the way, the truth, and the life: no man cometh unto the Father, but by me" (Jn. 14:6).

Jesus declares Himself to be the Truth, and therefore the only true Way of coming to the Father. In the latter, the Word of God is the expression of the Truth – Jesus Christ – as presented in the prayer of our Lord, the night He was betrayed, saying,

"Sanctify them through thy truth: thy word is truth" (Jn. 17:17).

Jesus and His Word are one; to know Truth as a Person, you must first know His Word. His Word brings you into a personal relationship with the Living Word – Jesus Christ. He denounced His Jewish audience for their unwillingness to know Him, saying,

"You search the scriptures, for in them you think you have eternal life; and these are they which testify of Me. But you are not willing to come to Me that you may have life" (Jn. 5:39 NKJV).

This passage serves as a stark warning to us not to study the Word as an end in itself but rather, as a means to end, which is to have a personal relationship with the Living Truth.

Truth in the realm of the Spirit is more real than truth in the natural realm. Why? Because truth is eternal, whereas natural truth is temporary and subject to change. Therefore, the Apostle Paul exhorts us to focus our attention on unseen realities rather than on things that are seen (2 Cor. 4:18). We do this by focusing our thoughts on God's Word which is a mirror into the unseen realm (2 Cor. 3:18). The invisible realm must take precedence, in the life of a believer, over the realm of the natural through walking by faith and not by sight (2 Cor. 3:7).

This natural realm was established by God for the normal course of things. But there is an unseen enemy who is a liar and deceiver, who uses the realm of the natural to manipulate and deceive, and if you live life merely from the natural – your physical senses, you will succumb to the deception and temptation of the devil. This was the very strategy Satan used, in the beginning, which caused Adam and Eve to fall into sin. He deceived Eve into doubting God's word - not to eat of the forbidden fruit. She focused on what the enemy wanted her to see with her physical eyes rather than what God said. The Bible said,

"And when the woman saw that the tree was good for food, and that it was pleasant to the eyes, and a tree to be desired to make one wise, she took of the fruit thereof, and did eat, and gave also unto her husband with her; and he did eat" (Gen. 3:6).

The above verse of scripture begins with her seeing that the tree was good for food – lust of the flesh; it was pleasant to the eyes – lust of the eyes; a tree desired to make her wise – pride of life. These three aspects of Eve's temptation are in the world today (see 1 Jn. 2:16). There are things that occur in this world that are true in the sense that they really exist but some things, though they exist, are not morally or ethically true because they contravene the divine Truth of God's Word. Everything we see or hear must be judged by the standard of what God said in His Word, for this is the spirit of wisdom:

"And the spirit of the LORD shall rest upon him, the spirit of wisdom and understanding...and he shall not judge after the sight of his eyes, neither reprove after the hearing of his ears: But with righteousness shall he judge..." (Is. 11:2a, 3b, 4a).

Also, Jesus, in denouncing His Jewish audience's erroneous

perception of Him, said,

"Judge not according to the appearance, but judge righteous judgment" (Jn. 7:24).

What we see with our physical sight is not always as it seems. For example, the sun rises at the beginning of the day, slowly moves across the sky and descends at the end of the day. Now, in reality, scientists expound that it is not the sun that moves across the sky, but rather, it is the earth which is moving in relation to the sun. So is it with the Christian life. See things from God's eternal perspective and live life from the realm of the Spirit by discerning between truth and error. This is at the very heart of spiritual warfare. The Christian is divinely summoned, to put on the complete armour of God; purpose: to stand against the wiles of the Devil,

"Put on the whole armour of God that ye may be able to stand against the wiles of the devil" (Eph. 6:11).

This passage of scripture tells us that our fight is not against the Devil *per se* but rather against his "wiles". What are "wiles"? Well, the English and the original Greek languages render the same meaning. "Wiles", according to the Collins Dictionary, is defined as trickery, cunning, craftiness; an artful or seductive trick; to lure, beguile or entice. The Greek rendering is "methodia" and it denotes craft, deceit, a cunning device, the craft of deceit; used in Ephesians 4:14 to "...lie in wait (to deceive). Satan's only weaponry is deception. He has no authority or power of his own. Whatever power he possesses, has been yielded to him through his lies and trickery. Anytime we give up our authority to Satan through his craftiness and enticements, he takes that authority and uses it against us; that is why the Apostle Paul warns the Church to "...give no place to the devil (Eph. 4:27). To the degree that you give him place, is the degree to which he will influence your life.

The only way to identify and overcome his lies and trickery is through the knowledge of the Truth; that truth tells us that we are more than conquerors through Christ who loved us (Rom. 8:37); we are partakers of the victory that Christ won for us in His sacrificial death and resurrection (Col. 2:14-15). Satan and his followers are defeated foes (Heb. 2:14), and if you understand this truth, he cannot gain the ascendancy in your life, but if you are ignorant of this fact, Satan will have the advantage according to Hosea 4:6: "My people are destroyed for lack of knowledge..."

The battleground where this warfare is waged between Truth and deceit is in the MIND; confirmed by God's Word:

"But I fear, lest by any means, as the serpent beguiled Eve through his subtlety, so your MINDS should be corrupted from the simplicity that is in Christ" (2 Cor. 11:3).

The number one thing Satan is after is your mind because if he can get your mind under his influence, he can control your life. God's stark warning to every believer is this:
"
"[guard] your heart with all diligence; for out it are the issues of life" (Prov. 4:23).

Shield your mind and heart with the Truth of God's Word through diligent study and meditation that equips you to act on it (Josh. 1:8). The psalmist describes God's Truth as our shield

The Shield of Truth

and buckler; part of a military arsenal for a soldier to use in distant combat (1 Sam. 17:7; 2 Chron. 11:12). In the Hebrew rendering, the word is "sinna" and it denotes a large shield that protects the soldier from flying missiles – arrows, spears, rocks, and other similar objects – which travel a long distance. I am reminded of one of the pieces of armour in Ephesians 6:16:

"Above all, taking the shield of faith, wherewith ye shall be able to quench the fiery darts of the wicked.

These fiery darts mentioned in this verse refer to Satan's lies and trickery that are hurled at us to deceive and destroy, but using the shield of faith will quench them.

Truth, in the passage of Psalm 91:4, is translated from the Hebrew word "emet", meaning firmness. Its Hebrew root is "aman", meaning to confirm, support, uphold, to be established, to be faithful, certain, to believe in; a certainty which is expressed in the definition of faith borne out in Hebrews 11:1. And so, the shield of truth can also be described as the shield of faith for two^sreasons:
) faith comes by hearing the Word of Truth (Rom. 10:17); 2) faith equals faithfulness (Heb. 2:4; Rom. 1:17; 3:3).

A buckler is generally understood to be a small shield used in close combat, or some similar kind of armour. We are encouraged to put on the whole armour of God (Eph. 6:11). Putting the armour on is to be done on the inside: clothing the inner man with the armour of light to prepare for close combat against the enemy (Rom. 13:12). What you clothe yourself with on the inside will be reflected on the outside, the outward man and his environment. Protection on the inside will result in protection on the outside. Revelation knowledge on the inside will cause the soul to prosper in what it knows, and therefore will create an atmosphere of prosperity on the outside. 3 John 2 states,

"Beloved, I wish (Gk pray) above all things that thou mayest prosper and be in health, even as thy soul prospereth."

The Apostle John in writing to the beloved Gaius, prays that he would prosper – success, accomplishments, victories – and health are proportionate to the prosperity of the inner man. Spiritual things work from the inside out, not vice versa. For example, financial prosperity does not begin in your pocket or bank account but in your soul. These benefits begin by feeding your spirit on the Word of God, for John goes on to further show us how Gauis was prospering in his soul:

"For I rejoiced greatly, when the brethren came and testified of the truth that is in thee, even as thou walkest in the truth" (3 Jn. 3).

To prosper in your soul, you must walk in the Truth by diligent study, meditation and application of God's Word to your life. The degree to which you prosper in your soul is the degree to which you will succeed in your life on earth. How does this change begin? Well, it begins in your mind. If you are going to live a fortified, successful Christian life, you must change the way you think. Joshua 1:8, tells us,

"This book of the law shall not depart out of thy mouth; but thou shalt meditate therein day and night, that thou mayest observe to do according to all that is written therein: for then thou shalt make thy way prosperous, and then thou shalt have good success."

This verse of scripture divulges the key to prosperity and success; it is meditation on God's Truth: the Word of God. And exercising your mind and mouth in His Word is what propels you to walk in Truth, for where your mind goes, your walk will follow:

"for they that are after the flesh do mind the things of the flesh; but they that are after the Spirit the things of the Spirit. For to be carnally minded is death; but to be spiritually minded is life and peace. For as he thinketh in his heart so is he..." (Rom. 8:5-6; Prov. 23:7a).

The mind is the doorway to the human heart, and this is Satan's ultimate goal; if you give him access to your mind, then he can control your walk. Your entertainment of Satan's thoughts, - lies and deceptions, will create strongholds in your heart. Conversely, your meditation on God's thoughts: the Word of God will build God's stronghold in your heart. Strongholds are fortresses of protection against the assaults of enemy attack. 2 Corinthians 10:4-5 gives us the process by which strongholds are constructed in the human mind:

"(for the weapons of our warfare are not carnal, but mighty through God to the pulling down of strongholds;) casting down imaginations, and every high thing that exalts itself against the knowledge of God, and bringing into captivity every thought to the obedience of Christ. And having in a readiness to revenge all disobedience, when your obedience is fulfilled."

First of all, the Apostle tells us that the battleground where these strongholds are built is in the mind, and the strongholds are composed of thoughts that you were taught or experiences you have had; ideologies, arguments, reasonings and perceptions that are in opposition to the knowledge of God's Word. Here is the progressive formation of strongholds that affect one's conduct and destiny in life: thoughts, imaginations, high things and strongholds (2 Cor. 10:4-5).

Satan's temptations begin with a thought. The Greek word for thought is "noema" and it refers to a design or purpose; that which is thought out. Satan's strategy is to put ungodly thoughts in your mind, but you can remove them by focusing on God's thoughts; in doing so, you refuse to entertain or dwell on thoughts that contradict the Word. However, if you take the enemy's thoughts and begin to meditate on them, you come to the next stage of imaginations.

Imaginations come from the Greek rendering: "logismos", a reasoning, and is suggestive of evil intent and mental contemplation of actions. It is a process of meditation on the desired action. In this meditation, that thing becomes an exalted thing.

The high thing – "hupsoma", in the Greek, refers to a mountain or anything of height. Metaphorically, it indicates anything to which a person attaches greater importance above the knowledge of God, becomes their god, whether money, friends or ungodly lifestyles. Whatever you exalt ends up becoming your stronghold, which equals bondage.

In the Greek, the word for stronghold is "ochuroma", and signifies a fortress. The term is akin to "ochuroo", to make firm, and is used metaphorically to indicate wrong thinking that has become established and rooted in the mind and heart of someone, tantamount to bondage. That bondage or habitual way of thinking can only be broken by the renewing of the mind (Rom. 12:2). Transformation occurs by renewing the mind in the Word of Truth. The mental process by which one falls into spiritual bondage is the same process by which one can be transformed through thoughts, imaginations, exaltation of godly things and then becoming a holy stronghold in your life.

5

Freedom From the Spirit of Fear

"Thou shalt not be afraid for the terror by night; nor for the arrow that flieth by day; Nor for the pestilence that walketh in darkness; nor for the destruction that wasteth at noonday" (Ps. 91:5-6).

In the opening passage of scripture, there are four things stated that we shall not be afraid of as we abide in the consciousness of His Presence - the terror by night, the flying arrow by day, the pestilence of the darkness and the noonday destruction. Because the Presence of God drives out fear, these calamitous things will not come upon those who trustfully abide under the shadow of His wings.

Where there is fear, there is also an open door for that evil, destructive calamity to enter in because fear is a force of attraction; the other force of attraction is faith. Faith is the opposite of fear; the latter is the antithesis of the former. Faith is the substance of good things desired, but fear, a reciprocal force, is the substance of evil things not desired. Fear can only be overcome by faith.

Without walking in faith, fear as a negative force will attract the things you do not desire. In the case of Job, he said,

"For the thing which I greatly feared is come upon me, and that which I was afraid of is come unto me. I was not in safety, neither had I rest, neither was I quiet; yet trouble came" (Job 3:25-26).

Here is Job's state of mind prior to the troubles coming upon him. His life was fraught with fear and terror. He had not just fear but great fear. Job did not feel safe, neither did he walk in rest nor quietness of spirit. Fear debilitated him, making him discouraged, weak and afraid of the things his fearful heart was focusing on.

On the other hand, David declared his confidence and boldness in God when he said,

"The LORD is my light and my salvation; whom shall I fear? The LORD is the strength of my life; of whom shall I be afraid" (Ps. 27:1).

David's boldness was the result of focusing on God as his Light, Salvation and Strength. When you focus on God who is good, there is no room for fear to enter. However, if your attention is on the evil, fear will come and dominate you. David's boldness came out of his relationship with God – meditating on His promises. The Bible tells us that he who trusts in the Lord shall not be afraid of evil tidings because his heart is fixed and established (Ps. 112:7).

According to the law of the spirit realm, the thing you fear will dominate you and have the mastery over your life. You will be a slave to that thing. Fear always brings bondage with it as the scripture states,

"...who through fear of death were all their lifetime subject to bondage" (Heb. 2:15).

Fear is bondage; it is a snare to the one who has it (Prov. 29:25). Whatever comes against you and you submit to fear, it is evidence that it has the power to destroy you. But if fear is absent because you are trusting the Lord, the things that come against you will have no power destroy you because fear is absent, thereby giving no access. King David had no fear, therefore his enemies could not defeat him since no fear was present to give his enemies the ascendancy. That is why David said in the next verses: Psalm 27:2-3,

"When the wicked, even my enemies and my foes, came upon me to eat up my flesh, they stumbled and fell. Though an host should encamp against me, my heart shall not fear: though war should rise against me, in this will I be confident."

King David was able to experience victory and protection from his enemies in verse 2 because the Lord was his Light, Salvation and Strength in verse 1. His mind was focused on God, therefore fear could not come in and persuade him to give up his authority which was there to protect his soul.
The greatest enemy against divine authority in a believer, is fear.

Fear brings intimidation in order to get the believer to give up his authority and when that happens, the hedge of protection is removed, then the enemy has access to steal, kill and destroy (Jn. 10:10). Evidence that authority has been given up to the adversary is that the person will experience weakness, discouragement and lack of confidence, resulting in making wrong decisions in life.

The remedy for fear is to stay your mind on the Lord as spoken by the Prophet Isaiah,

"Thou wilt keep him in perfect peace, whose mind is stayed on thee: because he trusteth in thee" (Is. 26:3)

How do you get your mind stayed on God? You do it by meditating on His Word – His good report for the believer. And that will keep you in perfect peace which, in the Hebrew, is shalom shalom: a double annunciation given to convey the depth, profoundness and greatness of God's peace; a peace that is unshaken in the most difficult of circumstances. His peace within us assures us that divine protection is inherent.

To live in divine peace, the Bible exhorts us to keep our minds focused on Him and His ability to deliver us from the terror and destruction of this fallen world. Jesus said,

"Let not your heart be troubled: ye believe in God, believe also in me...Peace I leave with you, my peace I give unto you: not as the world giveth, give I unto you. Let not your heart be troubled, neither let it be afraid" (Jn. 14:1, 27).

It is seen to be clear in this passage of scripture that fear, that is being afraid, troubles the heart. But Jesus tells us we can choose not to be troubled or afraid. How you do this? By believing in God and His Son, choose to believe in His Word, for peace is a product of faith, as it is written,

"Thou wilt keep him in perfect peace,...because he trusteth in thee. Therefore being justified by faith, we have peace with God through our Lord Jesus Christ" (Is. 26:3; Rom. 5:1).

Faith gives us peace in three aspects: peace with God; peace of mind and heart; and peace with others. In trusting God, He will keep us in perfect peace. Faith ministers peace but fear ministers doubt; it opens the door for doubt to enter into one's life. There is the spirit of faith (2 Cor. 4:13) and there is the spirit of fear (2 Tim. 1:7). These two opposite forces are fighting to have control in your life. In the incident of Peter walking on water, it shows how fear and doubt work together to render one ineffective in life.

After Jesus miraculously fed the five thousand with five loaves and two fish, He commanded His twelve disciples to get in a boat and go over to the other side, while He sent the multitude away and went up into a mountain to pray (Matt. 14:15-23). The disciples in the boat were tossed violently by the waves of the sea and the wind was boisterous. Then Jesus came to them walking on the water; the disciples were terrified, supposing it was a ghost, but Jesus assured them that it was Him.

At the point of this narrative, Peter presents a bold request to walk towards Jesus on the water. His reply to Peter was, to come. The story picks up from here, in Matthew 14:29-31,

"...And when Peter was come down out of the ship, he walked on the water, to go to Jesus. But when he saw the wind boisterous, he was afraid; and beginning to sink, he cried, saying, Lord, save me. And immediately Jesus stretched forth his hand, and caught him, and said unto him, O thou of little faith, wherefore didst thou doubt?"

Peter stepped out in faith on the word of Jesus and walked on the water. His faith gave him the ability to walk on water, with his focus on Jesus. As Peter was walking towards Jesus, he took his eyes off Him and on to the boisterous sea and violent winds. Instead of walking by faith on the water, he began to walk by sight. Then he began to sink – crying out in terror for the Lord to save him.

Jesus identified the problem in Peter to be doubt; the very reason why he began to sink. Furthermore, doubt entered into Peter through the door of fear, and fear overcame him because his focused attention was misplaced – he focused his eyes on the waging sea and boisterous winds, rather than Jesus, the Author and Finisher of our faith (Heb. 12:3).

Peter's walk of faith on the water began when he observed Jesus as his example walking on the water. He saw Jesus not merely with his physical eyes but with the eyes of his understanding. Peter understood that he could also walk on the water because he perceived Jesus as his example; so what Jesus did, he believed he could also do. As Jesus walked in authority over the violent waters of the sea, Peter was inspired to do the same because his spiritual eyes were on Jesus.

Everything Jesus did in His ministry was to show His disciples that they were able to do it as well, whether preaching the gospel, healing the sick, raising the dead, casting out devils or cursing the fig tree (Matt. 10:1,7-8; 17:20; 21:21-22; 1 Jn. 2:6). Jesus, as our example and focus, initiates our walk of faith (Heb. 12:3). Peter, seeing Jesus, requested to walk on the water to Him, and did so on the basis of His word, "Come."

As Peter walk in authority over the waves of the sea, he turned his eyes off Jesus and began to look to his circumstances. At this point, fear and intimidation entered in because Peter yielded his authority to fear, and therefore, it robbed him of his power to walk on water, thus resulting in him beginning to sink. His fear, as perverted faith, believed in the authority and power of the raging seas to destroy him. When you give up your authority, you give up your protection. What you fear will dominate you; what you are intimidated by will have power to hurt and harm you.

The person who maintains his authority will not be afraid of the terror by night, nor the arrow by day; neither will he be afraid of the deadly plagues that roam in darkness, "nor the destruction that lays wastes at noonday" (Ps. 91:5-6). When you know who you are in Christ, you will walk in your God-given authority.

Here are some principles to functioning in your authority over fear: Firstly, live in the consciousness that God's Presence is with you. The Lord said to Joshua, "...be not afraid, neither be dismayed: for the LORD thy God is with thee whithersoever thou goest" (Josh. 1:9). Feed your spirit, in the Word, on the fact that God will never leave us nor forsake. Meditate on scriptures that minister this truth (Matt.28:20; Jn. 14:17; Heb. 13:5). Secondly, Jesus Christ has delivered us from the fear of death when He gave His life, on our behalf, at the Cross of Calvary. The Bible states, "...through death he might destroy him that had the power of death, that is, the devil; And deliver them who through fear of death were all their lifetime subject to bondage" (Heb. 2:14-15). Fear and death entered the world through sin (Gen. 2:17; 3:9-11; Rom. 5:12). But when sin was destroyed in the body of Jesus, its fruit –fear and death – were eradicated from our lives. Destroying the root also destroys the fruit. Thirdly, it is not in our nature to fear as a new creation in Christ for two reasons: 1) old things are past away and all things have become new (see 2 Cor. 5:17); 2) the Word of God informs us, "For God hath not given us the spirit of fear; but of power, and of love, and of a sound mind" (1 Tim. 1:7). Your new spirit that you received when you were born again does not have fear (Ezek. 36:26) because it is born of the nature of the Holy Spirit (Jn 3:6, 8). Furthermore, when you receive the baptism with the Holy Spirit, you do not receive the spirit of bondage again to fear, but you receive the Spirit of liberty (Rom. 8:15; 2 Cor. 3:17). Fourthly, obedience to the Word liberates us from the bondage of fear for St John 8:31-32 states, "...if ye continue in my word, then are ye my disciples indeed; And ye shall know the truth, and the truth shall make you free." To continue in Christ's word means to obey His teaching and the one who hears and does His word, Jesus said, will be compared to a wise man who built his house upon a rock (Matt. 7:24). If disobedience brought the bondage of fear in the world, then obedience through faith will break the bondage of fear over your life. Lastly, pursue the love of God and walk in it, for perfect love expels all fear as the scripture states, "There is no fear in love; but perfect love casteth out fear: because fear hath torment. He that feareth is not made perfect in love" (1 Jn. 4:18).

Love is the antithesis of fear. Divine love is the motivation behind selflessness, but fear is fed and fuelled by self-centeredness. Self thinks about itself – what is in it for me? What am I going to lose if I do this? Fear thrives on self-centeredness, whereas love lays down its own life to fulfil the Will of God. Love is characterised, in 1 Corinthians 13, as not being selfish: "...seeketh not her own..." (v5b); nor boastful: "...vaunteth not itself..." (v4d); neither proud: "...is not puffed up" (v5e). The negative traits detailed above, belong to the self-centered life. Fear's chief-collaborator is self; that is why Jesus said,

"...If any man will come after me, let him deny himself, and take up his cross, and follow me. For whosoever will save his life shall lose it: and whosoever will lose his life for my sake shall find it" (Matt. 16:24-25).

Fear will motivate a man to save his own life to his own detriment, and on the other hand, prevent him from losing his own life for Christ's sake. So follow earnestly after love and live free from the spirit of fear.

6

In the World but not of this World

"A thousand shall fall at thy side, and ten thousand at thy right hand; but it shall not come nigh thee. Only with thine eyes shalt thou behold and see the reward of the wicked" (Ps. 91:7-8).

The above title of this chapter reminds me of the profound statement Jesus made in His prayer just before His hour of suffering:

"I pray not that thou shouldest take them out of the world, but that thou shouldest keep them from the evil. They are not of the world, even as I am not of the world" (Jn. 17:15-16).

Notice, Jesus didn't pray for His disciples to be taken or raptured out of this world because God's will was for them to fulfil their divine assignment as ambassadors on earth. The Lord's Prayer was an expression of the Father's will. And the Father's will was this: that they should be kept and protected from evil. So to put it in other words; God's perfect will is for His disciples to be insulated, not isolated – to be among the people of the world and be unaffected by the moral, spiritual and physical corruption that is in the world.

This notion is reflected in the Psalm that states: "A thousand shall fall at thy side and ten thousand at thy right hand; but it shall not come nigh thee" (Ps. 91:7). The reason why the thousand and ten thousand fall is because they are being rewarded for their sins whether by a direct judgment of God or by the law of sowing and reaping (Gal. 6:7-8), for the next verse says, "Only with thine eyes shalt thou behold and see the reward of the wicked" (v8). However, to the righteous, calamity will not come near.

In the Bible, it can be seen that the righteous Judge does not punish the righteous with the wicked, revealed in the judgment of Sodom and Gomorrah, the Egyptians and the Babylonian invasion. God puts a difference between the godly and the ungodly.

In Genesis 18:23-26 Abraham intercedes on behalf of Sodom and Gomorrah; the content of his conversation with the Lord reveals some interesting thoughts regarding how God judges a city and its inhabitants:

"And Abraham drew near, and said, wilt thou also destroy the righteous with the wicked? Peradventure there be fifty righteous within the city: wilt thou also destroy and not spare the place for the fifty righteous that are therein? That be far from thee to do after this manner, to slay the righteous with the wicked: and that the righteous should be as the wicked, that be far from thee: Shall not the Judge of all the earth do right? And the LORD said, If I find in Sodom fifty righteous within the city, then I will spare all the place for their sake."

Abraham's intercession before the Lord tells us that the presence of the righteous in a city is a preserving influence to that city and its inhabitants, from divine retribution. If there be fifty righteous, God declared, He would not destroy Sodom. This reminds me of Jesus' teaching: "Ye are the salt of the earth..." (Matt. 5:13). Abraham reiterated his request for Sodom regarding the forty-five righteous, then the forty, thirty, twenty, and ten righteous persons.

The conclusion of the matter was that there was not even found in Sodom five righteous persons. Therefore God poured out His wrath – fire and brimstone – upon Sodom and Gomorrah after the angels had brought out righteous Lot (Gen. 19:13-30; 2 Peter 2:6-8). In this, God did not punish the righteous with the wicked; this principle is seen repeatedly throughout the Word of God. Another example is when God preserved His people Israel, while the ten plagues fell upon the Egyptians as a result of Pharaoh's stubbornness not to let Israel go; the Lord separated the Israelites from the Egyptians. God's covenant-people were unaffected by the plagues. Just to give one example; God was about to bring a plague of flies upon Egypt and said,

"...Let my people go that they may serve me. Else, if thou wilt not let my people go, behold, I will send swarms of flies upon thee, and upon thy servants, and upon thy people, and into thy houses: and the houses of the Egyptians shall be full of swarms of flies, and also the ground thereon they are. And I will sever in that day the land of Goshen, in which my people dwell, that no swarms of flies shall be there; to the end thou mayest know that I am the LORD in the midst of the earth" (Ex. 8:20-22).

In this particular case, God purposely separated His people in Goshen from the Egyptians in all the Land of Egypt to show that He is the LORD in the midst of the earth. In the midrashic interpretation of the Old Testament, there are historic events and passages of scripture that have more than one fulfilment – an end time prophetic fulfilment – where God will pour the same kind of judgments in the last days, depicted in the Book of Revelation (7:7-9; 11:4-6; 16:1-4, 10). If God separated His covenant people from the ungodly in His divine judgments, He will do so again in these last days. The righteous, untouched, will see and behold the reward of the wicked (Ps. 91:8).

After the children of Israel were delivered from Egypt, God promised His people in the Old Testament that the evils that came upon Egypt would not come upon them if they obeyed Him:

"And said, If thou wilt diligently hearken to the voice of the LORD thy God, and wilt do that which is right in his sight, and wilt give ear to his commandments, and keep all his statutes, I will put none of these diseases upon thee, which I have brought upon the Egyptians: for I am the LORD that healeth thee" (Ex. 15:26).

"And the LORD will take away from thee all sickness, and will put none of the evil diseases of Egypt, which thou knowest, upon thee; but will lay them upon all them that hate thee" (Deut. 7:15).

These two passages of scripture show us that sicknesses and diseases belong to Egypt, not God's people. God therefore promised His people who were separated from Egypt, that He would take away every sickness from their midst and would not put any of the diseases of Egypt upon them.

In Biblical typology, Egypt is a type of the ungodly and worldly system, and so it is true today that diseases belong to this worldly system over which Satan presides as the god of this world. God's people who have been redeemed by the blood of Jesus Christ have been separated from that accursed system with its wickedness and curses. They do not belong to us for He promised not to put any of these curses upon us, but that He would put them upon those who hate us. God is not putting sickness upon us to make us more spiritual; sickness is of the Devil (Acts 10:38). God wants His people well!

There are also evils that come not as a result of direct divine retribution (Jn. 9:1-3), but because we live in a fallen world where the universal curse is in operation because of Adam's sin (Rom. 5:12-14). Accidents, barrenness, poverty, still births, birth deformities, sickness and diseases, just to name a few, permeate the whole world in every strata of society. Some experience these evils by the law of sowing and reaping on a natural level – poor diet, carelessness, lack of physical exercise, being in the wrong place at the wrong time or even circumstances beyond your control.

There is also sowing and reaping on a spiritual level such as sin, unforgiveness, hatred, lack of diligence in prayer and the ministry of the Word, neglecting to be led by the Spirit, unbelief, ignorance and religious tradition. And I believe the last two are foundational to why God's people fall short of God's provision of protection.

With respect to ignorance, the Bible states,

"My people are destroyed for lack of knowledge: because thou hast rejected knowledge, I will also reject thee,..." (Hos. 4:6a).

Destruction comes to God's people because of the lack of revelation knowledge concerning God's Word. Satan, the destroyer, thrives in an atmosphere of ignorance. Oh how untrue is this statement: *what you don't know won't hurt you;* no! What you do not know is killing you! Satan's authority to deceive, kill and destroy (Jn. 1.0:10) is enforced in the darkness (Col. 1:13; Eph. 6:12). Your darkness is your area of ignorance where the light of revelation knowledge is absent. In ignorance, you cannot appropriate what you do not know is yours. But once you come into the knowledge of the truth and accept it, the prince of darkness cannot overcome the Light (Jn. 1:5). You will know the truth and the truth will make you free (Jn. 8:31-32).
The enemy can only take advantage of you if you are ignorant of his devices (2 Cor. 2:11) and what rightfully belongs to you in Christ Jesus. That is why it is very important that every born again believer be an avid student of the Word of God, regardless of whether or not you are called into one of the fivefold ministry offices. You are required to study God's Word because you are a disciple and the word "disciple" in the Greek is "mathetes", meaning a learner, pupil, or student, and Jesus has called us to learn of Him (Matt. 11:29).

If a benefactor bequeaths a monetary inheritance to His son stipulated in his Will, and that son is ignorant of it, he will not enjoy what legally belongs to him. In the same vein, you can only appropriate God's inheritance including His protection through revelation knowledge of God's Word. 1 Peter 1:3 states,

"According as his divine power hath given unto us all things that pertain unto life and godliness, through the knowledge of him that hath called us to glory and virtue: Whereby are given unto us exceeding great and precious promises: that by these ye might be partakers of the divine nature, having escaped the corruption in the world through lust."

In the above text, the past tense verbs – "hath given" - are used to convey that God has already fulfilled His responsibility to us by Christ Jesus; He has given unto us all things in Christ. We have been blessed with all spiritual blessings in heavenly places in Christ (Eph. 1:3). God has provided everything we will ever need regarding life and godliness. But in order for it to become a realisation in our present world, we will need to acquire the revelation knowledge needed to appropriate what God has already given us. God is not withholding anything from us; it is our ignorance which is holding us back from receiving the things God has given us.

All things have been given unto us by God through the knowledge of Him concerning these exceedingly great and precious promises revealed in the Word of God. The Bible is replete with promises for the Christian to know and appropriate; and thus doing so, we become partakers of the divine nature – the incorruptible nature and life of God. This divine nature was deposited into us when we were born again. It is the incorruptible life of God. Through the exceedingly great and precious promises, the divine and incorruptible nature has been given to supplant the corruptible life, for 1 Peter 1:23 states,

"Being born again, not of corruptible seed, but of incorruptible, by the word of God, which liveth and abideth for ever."

The incorruptible nature resides in the seed of the Word of God by which we were born again. God's Word has the genetic code concerning who we are. Our new life is contrasted with the old life. Our new nature in Christ is incorruptible which in the Greek is "aphthartos", meaning "not liable to corruption, decay or destruction; the condition of becoming worse. Anything that causes destruction, decay or death, whether sin, depression, oppression, sickness, fear or accidents, fall under the law of corruption, but through participation in the divine nature, we escape the corruption in the world (2 Peter 1:4).

When you engage your mind and heart with the divine nature through the promises of God revealed in His Word, you will be delivered from the corruptive influences in the world. And God's nature - His incorruptible life in you will produce righteousness, peace, health, prosperity, renewed physical strength and vigour. This God-kind of life will not deteriorate, worsen or decay in the believer who embraces this truth. The Bible states,

"But the path of the just is as a shining light, that shineth more and more unto the perfect day" (Prov. 4:16).

God's will is that the righteous shine brighter and brighter in every area of their life; to live healthy and strong; to be sharp in one's mind because of the incorruptible nature of God in the believer.

The next thing that hinders the Christian from living out the divine life in him is religious tradition. When Jesus addressed the religious leaders regarding their man-made traditions, He said,

"howbeit in vain do they worship me, teaching for doctrine the commandments of men...Making the word of God of none effect through your traditions, which ye have delivered: and many such like things do ye" (Mk. 7:7, 13).

These traditions to which Jesus referred, were traditions that caused the people to contradict and violate the Word of God. For example, in the context of the passage, there was a tradition that contravened the commandment to honour father and mother (see Mk. 7:11-12). The religious leaders taught the people to say "corban," which means a gift; and in doing so, they were free from the responsibility of honouring their parents financially. This was one of many man-made traditions that was exalted above the authority of Scripture.

The word "tradition" is from the Greek rendering "paradosis", which literally means a handing down, and so, by metonymy, denotes the teachings of the Jewish rabbis in Mark 7: traditions are formulated by teaching, whether biblical or erroneous. It is the erroneous and man-made traditions that God's people need to guard against, for it is those traditions that make the Word of God powerless in a Christian's life (Mk. 7:13). Let us hold on to sound tradition that originates from the correct teaching of the Word of God.

In order to walk in the blessings of Psalm 91, you must guard against traditions such as "It is not always God's will to heal," or "God will not always protect His people from accidents or natural disasters," or "Sometimes God puts sickness upon you to teach you something," or "This sickness is for the glory of God," or praying, "If it be thy will" about a scriptural promise in the Word of God. These things will rob you of enjoying God's blessings in your life and showing the world that you are separate from its curses, so that,

"...all people of the earth shall see that thou art called by the name of the LORD;..." (Deut. 28:10).

This verse is mentioned in the passage on the blessings and how that these blessings shall come upon them and overtake them, that the world may know that Israel was called by His name. What was true of Israel then, is God's intention for His New Covenant people today. So live to your full potential and shine as lights in this dark world.

7

The Holy Spirit: our Habitation and Refuge

"**Because thou hast made the LORD, which is my refuge, even the most High, thy habitation,**" (**Ps 91:9**).

In several chapters earlier, the Scriptures stated that God is our refuge and dwelling place. Here, the same idea is conveyed in the above verse, that God is our refuge and habitation. The term "habitation is from the Hebrew word "mistor", and it signifies a place of shelter, whose Hebrew root means to hide or conceal. God is our hiding place, our shelter and refuge from evil. He protects and shelters through the presence and work of the Holy Spirit. Before proceeding further, we must understand who the Holy Spirit is. Is He merely a power or influence of God specifically taught by cults? Or is He more? Let us see what the Scriptures say about the Holy Spirit.

The Holy Spirit is mentioned at creation in the book of Genesis:

"In the beginning God created the heaven and the earth. And the earth was without form, and void; and darkness was upon the face of the deep. And the Spirit of God moved upon the face of the waters" (1:1-2).

The Spirit of God, who is also called the Holy Spirit (1 Cor. 3:16; 6:19; Acts 5:3, 9), was inherent in the creation of the world, performing His creative acts in response to the spoken words of God (Heb. 11:3; Job 33:4). If the Spirit of God created the heavens and the earth, that would affirm Him to be God Almighty, the Creator, the Omnipotent. To understand who is the Holy Spirit, it is important to first understand what the Bible says about the nature of God.

In John 4:24, Jesus spoke to the woman of Samaria concerning the nature of God and the nature of the worship that He requires of worshippers:

"God is a Spirit: and they that worship him must worship him in spirit and in truth."

Again in Isaiah 31:1, it states,

"Now the Egyptians are men, and not God; and their horses flesh, and not spirit."

These passages are telling us that the Egyptians are men and not God and their horses are flesh and not spirit. Men and horses are flesh but God is spirit. The nature and essence of God is invisible Spirit consisting of Father, Son and Holy Spirit (Matt. 28:19; Jn. 14:16). But when that divine nature manifests itself in its creative or powerful acts upon creation, it is personalised as Holy Spirit

(Job 33:4; Ps. 104:30; Is. 40:12-14).

To further understand the Holy Spirit and His work, it is needful to understand the triunity of God and the distinctive roles within the Godhead. The biblical definition of God's triune nature is this: God is one divine Spirit eternally manifested as Father, Son, and Holy Spirit; a plurality within the one divine essence or being called God – a unity of nature that is indivisible within the three "Persons" of the Godhead. The oneness of God is not a mathematical oneness but a qualitative oneness of essence and nature (Deut.6:4; Jn. 10:30).

In the work and economy of the Godhead, the Father, Son and Holy Spirit perform distinctive roles in the work of creation and redemption. The Father is the Source of the Godhead, who planned, initiated and decreed the creation of all things; foreordained the Way of redemption and the election of all the redeemed; and He is the initiator of divine revelation (Rom. 8:29-30; Eph. 1:3-4; 1 Peter 1:2, 19-20). God the Father has condescended from His divine invisible essence, to permanently and visibly localise Himself, in the likeness of a man, to sit on the throne of heaven, thus signifying His absolute power and authority over all creation (Is. 6:1; Rev. 4:2-6). Jesus Christ, the Son of God, the Word made flesh, is the revealer of the Father's plans and purposes on the earth; that is why He is called the Logos in Greek, which is translated "Word" (Jn. 1:1, 14, 18). As the Father decreed the world into existence, the Word spoke the worlds into existence and by that same Word all things are sustained and upheld (Heb. 1:2-3; 11:3; Jn. 1:3). As the Father is the Source of revelation, Jesus Christ is the mediator and expression of that revelation from God to humanity.

In the work of redemption, The Word of God was robed with flesh in the person of Jesus Christ; He died as a sacrifice for our sins, legally providing redemption and satisfying the righteous demands of God's Law that was against us. He was resurrected from the dead and ascended to sit on the right hand of His Father, continually making intercession for us (Rom. 8:32,34; Heb. 1:3). Now Jesus Christ is in heaven seated at the right hand of God in His glorified humanity, and will forever be the God-man: Christ Jesus (1Tim. 2:5).

The title "Holy Spirit", designates His character and nature. He is absolutely holy and pure, whose personality transcends every created being and object. He possesses holiness to the same degree as the Father and the Son, and so His Presence should be reverenced and feared. As to His nature, He is pure invisible Spirit. Whilst the Father has condescended to permanently manifest Himself on a throne in heaven, and the Son to remain the incarnate God-man at His right hand, the Holy Spirit will continue to exist as pure invisible Spirit to remind us that God in His true nature permeates and transcends the heavens and the earth, for He is not described as being seen in the eternal state of the righteous (Rev. 21-22).

The Holy Spirit is described as the third "person" of the Godhead for two reasons: firstly, this how He is positioned in the Great Commission of Matthew 28:19; secondly, he holds the closest relationship to creation in the work and economy of the Godhead. The Father relates to humanity through His Son (Col. 1:15-16; Heb. 1:2-3); Jesus, the Son of God relates to us through the Spirit (Jn. 14:26; 15:26; 16:13-15), but the Holy Spirit relates directly with God's creation and is therefore is the Agent of God's power and presence.

In the work of creation, God created the heaven and the earth in Genesis 1:1, and then shows us in verse 2 that He created by the Spirit of God moving upon the face of waters. In the Hebrew language, the word for "moved" is "rahap" and it signifies to brood over with a feeling of tender loving care; hence, to cherish. This term is used of an eagle brooding (fluttering) over her young (see Deut. 32:11), and so in like manner, the Spirit of God was brooding and hovering over the earth; His presence brings things into existence at the command of God's word (Job 33:4; Ps. 104:30).

Another word which could be used for brooding is "overshadow", so we can say that the Spirit of God overshadowed the face of the water – poised to do His creative acts of power upon the earth. He is the One in the Godhead who actually creates and works miracles when He comes upon something or someone. He is the manifest Presence of God on earth, the expression of the fullness of the Godhead.

The Holy Spirit is the Presence of God that broods and overshadows a person in the performance of His miracles. In the imminent conception of the Son of God, the angel Gabriel came to a virgin, called Mary, to announce her selection to conceive and give birth to the Son of God. The angel told her how she was going to conceive a child without human involvement. He said,

"...The Holy Ghost shall come upon thee, and the power of the Highest shall overshadow thee: therefore also that holy thing which shall be born of thee shall be called the Son of God" (Lk. 1:35).

According to the above verse, the angel related to her that the miraculous conception of the Son of God was to be the result of the Holy Spirit and His power overshadowing her. It was the Holy Spirit brooding over her like an eagle with her young that caused a miraculous conception to take place. Jesus Christ was a child of the Holy Ghost (Matt. 1:18, 20). The Spirit is the proximate Source of life for all living things.

To abide under the shadow of the Almighty is to remain under the wings of the Holy Spirit. God's Word states,

"Keep me as the apple of the eye, hide me under the shadow of thy wings" (Ps. 17:8).

It is the Holy Spirit who broods over us and covers us under the shadow of His wings. The Bible describes the Holy Spirit coming upon us as He did when the Son of God was conceived in the womb of the virgin Mary (Lk 1:35). In Acts 1:8, Jesus declared to His disciples:

"But ye shall receive power, after that the Holy Ghost is come upon you: and ye shall be witnesses unto me..."

Receiving power is the result of the Holy Spirit coming upon you – overshadowing you. This is the baptism with the Holy Spirit; an experience described as the Spirit coming upon the believer, and the Spirit in the believer (Jn. 14:17). It is also identified in Scripture as being and walking in the Spirit (Gal. 3:2-3; Rom. 8:9)

In the Old Testament, the Spirit of God came upon individuals, overshadowing and empowering them to perform supernatural or great exploits for God (Judges 13:25; 14:5-6; 1 Sam. 10:6,10). At

Jesus' baptism, the Bible states,

"...lo, the heavens were opened unto him, and he saw the Spirit of God descending like a dove, and lighting upon him" (Matt. 3:16b)

The Spirit of God is described descending like a dove upon Jesus. This description does not refer to the bodily form in which He came but rather, the manner in which He descended on Jesus. Notice the imagery of a bird is used to describe the Spirit's descent.

The Holy Spirit is the manifest Presence of God – that secret place, refuge, habitation and shadow of His wings. We inhabit God and God inhabits us by His Spirit. The Bible states,

"...And hereby we know that he abideth in us, by the Spirit which he hath given us. Hereby know we that we dwell in him, and he in us, because he hath given us of his Spirit" (1 Jn. 3:24b; 4:13).

According to these verses, God dwells in us and we dwell in Him by the Spirit He has given unto us. In other words, the Holy Spirit is our habitation – our dwelling place – and our bodies are His dwelling place – His temple (1 Cor. 3:16-17; 6:19; Eph. 2:22).

We are called as believers to live and walk in the Spirit – that is abide and be at home in the Spirit, for it is in the Spirit that we experience the love and fellowship of the Father and His Son. When we spend time having communion with the Holy Spirit, we are also having fellowship with the Father and His Son, Jesus Christ (2 Cor. 13:14; 1Jn. 1:3).

Everything I am sharing with you about the secret place will only be experienced in the Presence of the Holy Spirit. The Father and Jesus Christ His Son will only relate to you in the Person of the Holy Spirit. To experience the fullness of intimacy in the secret place, you must be baptised with the Holy Spirit or else your experience with God will be limited. Jesus said to His disciples,

"I have yet many things to say unto you, but ye cannot bear them now" (Jn. 16:12).

There are many Christians who are in the same situation as Jesus' disciples: they were made clean through the Word Jesus had spoken unto them; they left everything to go and follow Him; they even had the Holy Spirit with them, but Jesus exclaimed a very profound truth that the Spirit of God was going to be in them (Jn. 14:16-17; 15:3). This was key to them understanding and walking in divine power.

After Jesus conveyed to them that there were things they would not be able to bear, He continued to say in verse 13,

"Howbeit when he, the Spirit of truth, is come, he will guide you into all truth: for he shall not speak of himself; but whatsoever he shall hear, that shall he speak: and he will show you things to come."

As the Father is the Source of revelation, and the Son mediates that revelation; the Holy Spirit is the illuminator of that revelation from the Father and the Son (see Jn. 16:14-15). He illuminates the hearts of men concerning the revelation of redemption, and when a person receives it, the Holy Spirit imparts new life into that person's spirit through the new birth (Jn. 3:3-8; Titus 3:5).

Then that person is ready to receive the indwelling Presence of the Holy Spirit to inhabit him, and for he to inhabit the Spirit: our refuge and habitation. And that is why the passage in Romans 8:9 states,

"But ye are not in the flesh, but in the Spirit, if so be that the Spirit of God dwell in you..."

In the new birth, you begin your life in Christ (2 Cor. 5:17), but in the baptism with the Holy Spirit, you begin your life in the Spirit because He has come to indwell you (Gal. 3:2-3). And so yielding to the Spirit will connect you to a deeper understanding of Truth and a deeper intimacy with God.

Baptism with the Holy Spirit is an immersion into the Presence of the Holy Spirit from the inside out. While being filled on the inside, you are immersed in His Presence. It is like putting an empty glass in water; when immersed in the water, it is also filled up inside the glass. So it is with the baptism with the Holy Spirit. That realm of the Holy Spirit is our refuge, dwelling place and protection from the lusts and works of the flesh. The Apostle Paul exhorts us:

"This I say then, Walk in the Spirit, and ye shall not fulfil the lust of the flesh" (Gal. 5:16).

This scripture gives the correct order for a successful Christian life. The passage begins with the command to walk in the Spirit and only then, you will not fulfil the lust of the flesh that eventually reaps corruption (2 Peter 1:4). Notice, it did not say at the outset, **not** to fulfil the lust of the flesh so that you may walk in the Spirit. You see, some Christians think in this manner, and it is the reason they are living defeated lives.

Life in the Spirit is your habitation and refuge from the storms of life. There are Christians who take counsel, but not from God, and take cover but it is not the covering of His Spirit (Is. 30:1). Now it is time to take counsel from Him, and to come under the covering of His Spirit and begin to live life in Him.

There are specific principles to walking in the Spirit that I want to touch on.

Firstly, endeavour to be baptised with the Holy Spirit with the evidence of speaking in tongues, for this is the doorway to supernatural life in the Spirit (Acts 1:8; 2:1-4; Rom 8:9; Gal. 3:2-3). Secondly, earnestly desire the deeper infilling of the Spirit by speaking to yourself in psalms, hymns and spiritual songs making melody with your heart in worship to the Lord (Eph. 5:18-20).

Thirdly, spend quality time building up your inner man by praying daily in the Spirit, which is praying in tongues. This is a very efficient way of attuning your spirit to follow the promptings and direction of the Holy Spirit (1 Cor. 14:2, 14-16, 18; Eph. 6:18; Jude 1:20). Fourthly, study correctly the Word of God and get acquainted with the thoughts of the Holy Spirit who is the Author of the Bible which contains His thoughts (2 Tim. 2:15; 3:16-17; 2 Peter1:19-21). Lastly, to walk after the Spirit, set your mind, your thoughts and meditation on the things of the Spirit. Daily meditate, ponder and reflect also with the mouth, the mysteries of God's Word, for as a man thinks in his heart so is he (Prov. 23:7). Where the mind goes, the person follows. Whatever your mind reflects on, your walk will mirror (Josh. 1:8; Rom. 8:5-

6; 1 Tim. 4:15). Make bold confessions about your life in the Spirit; this will enable you to adjust and progress in your spiritual life and further activate the work of the Spirit in you. The Holy Spirit responds to spoken words that are in agreement with the Word of God (Heb. 12:5-6; 10:19, 23; Jn. 6:63).

God desires your whole spirit, soul and body to be saturated with the life, power and presence of the Holy Spirit, to the point that no sickness, diseases, viruses nor infection can infiltrate your body. The Apostle Paul said,

"But if the Spirit of him that raised up Jesus from the dead dwell in you, he that raised up Christ from the dead shall also quicken [make alive] your mortal bodies by his Spirit that dwelleth in you" (Rom. 8:11).

The Spirit of God wants to be a refuge and a habitation to your mortal body so that His Life is the principle by which you live your life in this present world. Jesus said in Mark's account of the Great Commission concerning those who believe, "if they drink any deadly thing, it shall not hurt them..." (Mk. 16:18b). When the Apostle Paul, the other prisoners and Roman soldiers shipwrecked on the Island called Melita, he was gathering sticks for the fire and a venomous snake fastened itself to Paul's hand, but he shook off the serpent into the fire and felt no harm (Acts 28:1-5). Paul's body was saturated with divine life that no deadly poison could harm him. It also reminds me of what Jesus said,

"Behold, I give unto you power to tread on serpents and scorpions, and over all the power of the enemy: and nothing shall by any means hurt you" (Lk. 10:19).

Moses, the servant of God, was one hundred and twenty years old when he died, his eyes were not dim neither did his natural strength diminish (Deut. 34:7). The law of the Spirit of life was coursing through his veins, organs and muscles so that his health and physical strength were maintained unto the day of his death. He did not die of any sickness or disease; God called him home by taking the breath of life from him. This also happened to Aaron the high priest (see Num. 20:23-29). With Joshua and Caleb, their physical strength was not decreased but both entered the Promised Land and fought the giants and the inhabitants at age eighty and eighty-five years (Josh. 14:6-14). If they experienced unabated strength under the Old Covenant, how much more should the New Covenant believers walk in the same strength, who live under a better Covenant established upon better promises (Heb. 8:6)

John G. Lake, a missionary from the United States, travelled to South Africa during the early years of the twentieth century. He went with a group of doctors to where a deadly plague was killing a large population. There was a dead body with foam from its mouth. John G. Lake took up with his hand some of the foam from the corpse's mouth and examined it under a microscope; the germ cells were still alive in his hand. However, when he handed the foam back to the scientists, the germs were all dead. They questioned how he could do this. John G. Lake replied, "The law of the Spirit of life in Christ Jesus has made me free from the law of sin and death" (Rom. 8:2). He walked in the midst of this deadly plague, while others died, he was not affected because he believed that no evil could befall him neither any plague could come near his dwelling (Ps. 91:10). Let the Holy Spirit take over your whole spirit, soul and body (1 Thess. 5:23) by being filled with the Spirit, allowing His life to course through your organs, veins and blood for the Spirit that raised up Jesus from the dead will rejuvenate your whole body to walk in divine health (Rom. 8:11; Ps. 103:5; Job 33:25).

8

Jesus Christ: our Passover Lamb

"There shall no evil befall thee, neither shall any plague come nigh thy dwelling" (Ps. 91:10)

Passover is a Jewish pilgrimage feast that was observed on the fourteenth day, Nisan. The term "Passover" in the Hebrew is "pesach; its verb form is pasach, meaning "to pass over". Its Greek equivalent is "pascha", which is used to refer to the lamb or the feast (Matt. 26:17). This feast was instituted by Moses under the commandment of God to preserve Israel's firstborn from the deadly plague when the Lord would pass through Egypt to smite the firstborn of the Egyptians. But with the Israelites, the Lord would pass over them, hence the name of the feast: Passover.

The historical account of the beginning of the feast is told in Exodus chapters 12 and 13. Having indepth knowledge about the Passover will help us to understand and appreciate what it means when Jesus Christ is said to be our Passover:

"Purge out therefore the old leaven, that ye may be a new lump, as ye are unleavened. For even Christ our Passover is sacrificed for us" (1 Cor. 5:7).

Apostle Paul briefly summarises the Passover feast, showing us that Jesus Christ is the fulfilment of the Old Testament feast. This feast was only a type or shadow of the true and good thing that was to come. That is why the Bible states,

"Let no man therefore judge you in meat, or in drink, or in respect of an holy day, or of the new moon, or of the Sabbath days: Which are a shadow of things to come; but the body is of Christ...For the law having a shadow of good things to come, and not the very image of the things, can never with those sacrifices which they offered year by year continually make the comers thereunto perfect" (Col. 2:16-17; Heb. 10:1).

The Apostle Paul's brief summary is based upon the assumption that his readers are already acquainted with the Old Testament. You need the understanding of both the Old and New Testaments to be mature in your understanding concerning what Jesus Christ did for us. That is why I going to point out the main features of Passover and how they reflect the true reality of redemption in Christ. Once the true reality has come, then the type or shadow is done away with. We no longer need to practise this feast but we do need to understand it so as to have a full revelation of what it signifies to accept Jesus as our Passover Lamb (1 Cor. 5:7).

Passover marks the beginning of the religious new year in Israel

(Ex. 12:1-2. Similarly, the Sacrifice of Jesus signifies the beginning of new life for everyone who puts their faith in Him (Rom. 6:4; 7:5-6; 2 Cor. 5:17). Why? Because God delivered His people from the bondage or slavery of Egypt to a life of freedom (Ex. 20:1-2) Even so, Christ as our Passover Lamb has delivered us from the bondage of sin (Jn. 8:31-36), and so presents the purpose of Passover. In addition, Passover commemorates the deliverance of Israel's firstborn from the Judgement of the deadly plague (Ex. 11:4-7; 12:12-13). In the same vein, through the blood of the Lamb of God, every believer in Christ has become God's firstborn, according to Hebrews 12:23, which tells us in the original Greek that we are the church or assembly of the firstborn ones, sanctified – set apart – unto God and delivered from the judgment of God's wrath (Ex. 13:12-15; Jn. 3:36; Rom. 5:9). This deliverance would mark the starting point of the Hebrew nation – God's holy nation, His peculiar people, a kingdom of priests (Ex. 19:5-6). Similarly, through the sacrifice of Jesus Christ, our Passover Lamb, God has purchased for Himself a chosen generation, a royal priesthood, a holy nation and a peculiar people to show forth His perfections in this dark and evil world (1 Peter 2:9; Eph. 5:26-27).

In Biblical typology, the similar features presented in the type or shadow must also be seen in its antitype – the true reality (Heb. 9:23-24). Jesus Christ fulfilled the main features and characteristics of the Old Testament Passover. The characteristics are as follows: the Passover lamb had to be without blemish (Ex. 12:5); Jesus Christ is identified as the sinless, spotless, unblemished Lamb of God (Heb. 9:14; 1 Peter 1:19-20). Without sin, sickness or any physical infirmity; qualified as God's perfect Sacrifice (Lev. 22:20-25).

Jesus Christ: our Passover Lamb

As the paschal lamb was killed in the evening (Ex. 12:6, Jesus Christ was crucified and died at evening. In the literal Hebrew, it is rendered "between the evenings." The Passover lamb was actually killed between the evenings which signified the point at which the sun began to decline and its full sun setting – between 3:00 PM to 6:00 PM (Edersheim 1995). Jesus died at the ninth hour (3:00 PM) on the fourteenth day of the month Abib, about the time that the Passover lambs were being sacrificed at the Jewish Temple (Ex. 12:6). Jesus fulfilled the time line of the Passover lamb.

The whole Passover lamb was to be roasted with fire, not cooked with water, so that not a bone of it should be broken (Ex. 12:46; Num. 9:12). Jesus fulfilled the type and shadow of the Passover lamb, for not a bone in His body was broken (Ps. 34:20; Jn. 19:32-36).

The whole sacrifice, when roasted, was to be eaten; however, if any remained until the morning, it was burnt with fire (Ex. 12:10). Because it was holy to God, none of it could remain and therefore needed to be burnt so that none of it experienced physical decay or corruption. This foreshadowed Jesus Christ, God's most holy sacrifice, who died, rose again from the dead and saw no corruption (Acts 2:30-31).

Time will not permit me to expound on all the other aspects of the Passover feast, so I want to come to a very important element of the sacrificial lamb, and that is its blood. God, through Moses, commanded the Israelites to take the blood of the Passover lamb and strike the two side posts and upper lintel. Notice, God did not command them to strike on the ground or threshold in order to serve as a stark reminder throughout the ages not to, with contempt, trample under foot the Son of God and the blood of His Covenant (Heb. 10:29).

The blood of the Passover lamb was the very thing that stopped the destroyer from entering in, for the Lord said,

"And the blood shall be to you for a token upon the houses where ye are: and when I see the blood, I will pass over you, and the plague shall not be upon you to destroy you, when I smite the land of Egypt...For the LORD will pass through to smite the Egyptians; and when he seeth the blood upon the lintel, and on the two side posts, the LORD will pass over the door, and will not suffer the destroyer to come in unto your houses to smite you" (Ex. 12:13, 23).

Here we see to protective power of the blood, of which the Passover sacrifice emphasises. The blood was sprinkled by faith around the door which signified the means of entrance or access to their dwelling, and that stopped the destroyer from entering in. The One Who needed to see the blood was God Himself, the Executor of divine judgment. It typifies Jesus Christ our Passover Lamb, whose blood was shed for us at Calvary to redeem us from the curse of death (Gal. 3:13-14). Through that blood, our door of access is covered so that the destroyer cannot enter in; however, it is our responsibility to ensure that our door is protected by the blood of Christ.

The Bible informs us not to give the devil any place (Eph. 4:27). This is vividly depicted in the biblical narrative of Cain and Abel (Gen. 4). Abel offered a more excellent sacrifice than Cain (Heb. 11:4). Cain offered of the produce of the ground. Abel's offering was accepted because he offered by faith, a blood sacrifice, whereas Cain offered the fruit of his hard labour – an offering unacceptable to God because the ground was cursed (Gen. 3:17; 5:28-29). Because of not offering a blood sacrifice, God informed him that sin was now waiting near his door of access to gain mastery over him (Gen. 4:7). Cain remained unrepentant, the sin of murder entered in and he killed his brother Abel. The principle of this story teaches us that hard religious toil and labour will never be acceptable before God; it is only faith in the blood sacrifice of Jesus that pleases God. The Bible states that we are accepted, by faith, in His beloved Son (Eph. 1:6-7; Heb. 11:6).

Keep the door of your life covered with the precious blood of Jesus by meditating and making confessions about what the Blood has already done for you and rest in that truth (Heb. 3:7-4:11). Cease from your own works and self-effort; focus your attention on the finished work of Calvary and enter the Rest through faith in His blood. Then perform the good works you have been ordained to walk in (Eph. 2:10), not to be saved, but because you are saved.

What does the blood of the Passover lamb mean in both the Old and New Testaments? Let us begin to answer it and unveil its power in the atoning work of Christ. There are three important aspects that will help us understand its efficacy: Its significance, value and power.

THE SIGNIFICANCE OF THE BLOOD

Why is the blood so important in the Levitical sacrificial system?

First of all, Leviticus 17:11 sheds light on this, saying,

"For the life of the flesh is in the blood: and I have given it to you upon the altar to make an atonement for your souls for it is the blood that maketh an atonement for the soul."

This verse intimates that the physical life of all flesh is in the blood; if the blood is drained out from any living thing, whether human life or animal life, physical death will occur. Therefore the shedding of blood is used to denote the occurrence of death or loss of life. And so in sacrificial terms, signifies the giving up of life through death, on behalf of another. In this case, blood is a metonymy for death. Why death? The Bible tells us that the wages of sin is death (Rom. 6:23; 5:12; Gen. 2:16-17). A person who disobeys God's righteous Law incurs the penalty of sin, which is death. Whoever sins come under the wrath of God's judgement, because God, who is holy cannot compromise with sin, or else He will be violating His own righteous character.

But thank God that He is love and mercy, and therefore has made provision for mankind to be freed from the penalty of death through God's own perfect sacrifice: Jesus Christ (Jn. 1:29). He came and died in our place so that we would have eternal life in Him. This truth is illustrated and taught in the sacrificial system set up by God in the Old Testament. The blood upon the altar signifies the life of a pure, innocent victim giving up in death on behalf of a sinner/worshipper. The blood makes an atonement (Heb. Kippur: covering) for the soul (Heb. Nephesh: life, person).

In retrospect, the Passover lamb was killed first, then its blood was sprinkled on the two side posts and upper lintel to signify

Jesus Christ: our Passover Lamb

the death of an innocent victim (Ex. 12:6-7, 21-23). The shedding of blood has no significance to God without the death of a sacrificial victim. So when we talk about the blood of Jesus - the blood of the Cross – we are speaking about His sufferings and death (Phil. 2:8; Col. 1:20).

As to the Passover lamb's substitutionary nature, a lamb was selected for a house: a family (Ex. 12:3, 21) and when the deadly plague of the firstborn passed through Egypt, all the firstborn of Israel in their houses were spared because an innocent sacrificial victim had already died in their place and the blood upon the door posts and lintel testified to this fact. In the same vein, our Passover Lamb: Jesus Christ, died in our place and His blood upon us testifies that we are no longer under the cures of death, its deadly plagues or evils, for no evil shall befall us, neither shall any plague come near our dwelling (Ps. 91:10). Jesus took all our sicknesses, diseases, poverty, oppressions and evils upon Himself (Is. 53:3-5; Matt. 8:16-17; 2 Cor. 8:9; 9:8).

Our dwelling of which no plague can come near, can be interpreted in a threefold sense: 1) God as our dwelling place; 2) our physical bodies that houses the real "you"; and 3) the homes in which we live. Through the blood, we are covered and protected.

THE VALUE OF THE BLOOD

The blood of Jesus has value, as recorded in 1 Peter 1:18-19:

"Forasmuch as ye know that ye were not redeemed with corruptible things, as silver and gold, from your vain conversation received by tradition from your fathers; but with the precious blood of Christ, as of a lamb without blemish and without spot" (1 Peter 1:18-19).

We were not redeemed or bought back with corruptible things as silver and gold, but we were bought with the price of the precious blood of Christ – an eternal redemption and inheritance (Heb. 9:12,15) that did not come from the vain practices and tradition of Jewish fathers. There are three essential truths, you need to know, that made the blood of Jesus Christ precious and efficacious to take away sin: 1) Christ's humanity; 2) His moral purity; and 3) His Divinity.

It was not sufficient that the blood of animals could take away sins; they were only types and shadows of the true sacrifice to come (Heb. 9:12-13; 10:1-4). Since it was a man who brought sin and death into the world, it could only take a man to liberate us. To buy back something, which is the meaning of redemption, would require an above or equivalent value. However, animal sacrifices were not of an equivalent value to redeem mankind from sin, for men are of a higher value than animal sacrifices because of being created in the image of God (Matt. 12:11-12; Gen. 5:1; Jam. 3:9). So God Himself partook of the nature of man - flesh and blood - to become the seed of Abraham, for the suffering of death (Heb. 2:14-15; Jn. 1:1-3, 14).

Jesus Christ was pure and sinless; the Bible says He was tempted in every point as we are, yet without sin (Heb. 4:15; 1 Peter 2:22-23). When He was put on trial before Pilate and Herod, they conclude that there was nothing in Him that was worthy of death (Matt. 27:23; Lk. 23:4, 13-15). When Judas, the betrayer, saw that the chief priests and elders conspired to put Jesus to death, and sending him to Pilate the governor said, "...I have sinned in that I have betrayed the innocent blood..." (Matt. 27:4). He said this when he saw that Jesus was condemned to death (Matt. 27:1-3). He used the phrase "innocent blood" in two ways: 1) a metonymy for impending death by execution; 2) a synecdoche – a part representing the whole – to refer to an innocent man. Jesus lived a perfect sinless life before God and man which gave His blood sacrificial value in the sight of God.

The blood of Christ was Divine because of whose blood it was. In Acts 20:28b, it affirms,

"...feed the church of God, which he hath purchased with his own blood."

It states that the blood with which the Church was purchased was God's own blood. Jesus Christ is the Word that was in the beginning with God and that Word was essentially called God (Jn. 1:1-2). That Word called God became flesh and tabernacled among us; being given the name Jesus, meaning salvation, he saved us from our sins by shedding His blood on a cross to purchase a people for Himself (Matt. 1:21; Jn. 1:14; 1 Tim. 3:16). Jesus Christ was a person with two natures: Divine and human.

As a synecdoche – where the blood stands for the person – His blood was not only human but also Divine, and this is what makes it of infinite value in the sight of God. Due to its infinite value, the blood of Jesus will never lose its power, giving us an eternal redemption that will last for ever and ever. Because of its Divine and infinite value, Jesus only needed to offer Himself once for us; unlike the blood of bulls and goats offered repeatedly every year which could never take away sin.

"...we are sanctified through the offering of the body of Jesus Christ ONCE for all" (Heb. 10:10).

To purchase for us a redemption that would last for all eternity through the offering of His body once for all, required a sacrifice to be infinite and eternal in value or else Jesus would need to have offered Himself repeatedly. But a one-off payment for our sins was sufficient. This gives the blood of Jesus infinite power over sin and death.

THE POWER OF THE BLOOD

When a strong man armed keepeth his palace, his goods are at peace: but when a stronger than he shall come upon him, and overcome him, he taketh from him all his armour wherein he trusted, and divideth his spoils" (Lk. 11:21-22).

The equivalent verse in the Gospel of Matthew states,

"Or else how can one enter into a strong man's house, and spoil his goods, except he first bind the strong man? And then he will spoil his house" (Matt. 12:29).

Jesus presents to the Pharisees the true reality of spiritual conflict between the two opposing kingdoms: the Kingdom of God and the kingdom of Satan. The Kingdom of God seeks to liberate men from spiritual bondage and the tyranny of Satan

(Acts 10:38). Conversely, the kingdom of darkness aims to enslave men; to steal, kill, and destroy (Jn. 10:10; 2 Tim. 2:26). Jesus makes it very clear to the religious leaders, when they accused Him of expelling demons by the power of Satan, that these two kingdoms, the Kingdom of God and the kingdom of darkness, are diametrically opposed in their mission, and therefore should not be confused (Matt. 12:22-28).

According to Mark 3:22, Jesus responded, to their false accusations, in parables, and the verses quoted above are part of the parable. Parables are earthly narratives or maxims that convey or reflect spiritual and ethical truths in the realm of the spirit. The strong man who is armed and keeps his palace is the Devil, but the stronger than he is Jesus Christ who comes, binds that strong man, strips him of his armour and weaponry, and takes away his spoils. Jesus first bound Satan and then plundered his kingdom. You may ask where and when did He do this? Well, look at what Colossians 2:14-15 states:

"Blotting out the handwriting of ordinances that was against us, which was contrary to us, and took it out of the way, nailing it to his cross; And having spoiled principalities and powers, he made a shew of them openly, triumphing over them in it."

The verse informs us that God in Christ blotted out (Gk exaleipho: wipe out) washed away, smeared over completely, removed away, obliterated the handwriting of ordinances, referring to the Law that was against us demanding our punishment and death, because of sin. He paid the debt that was justly required of us; God nailed the Law, the debt note, to His Cross. Jesus, having paid the debt of sin demanded by the Law, spoiled, plundered and stripped satanic principalities and powers, making a public display of them and triumphing over them by His Cross, that is, His death on the Cross (Col. 2:15). By His death, principalities and powers were stripped of their armour and weaponry (Lk. 11:21-22). His death paralysed him who had the power of death; that is the Devil (Heb. 2:14-15).

The blood of Jesus unleashed its power against the kingdom of darkness and overcame it at the moment He died. He bound and spoiled the enemy's kingdom; this is why Jesus' blood is so powerful because it testifies of His victory over the Devil, and the believers' union with Christ makes them partakers of that victory and triumph (2 Cor. 2:14; 1 Jn. 4:4). In plundering the satanic kingdom, Jesus has distributed the spoils of His death with the strong (Is. 53: 12; Dan. 11:32). The spoils or benefits of His victorious warfare, by the shedding of His blood on the Cross, has been distributed to us.

We are justified, sanctified and regenerated by His blood; have victory over Satan and his cohorts of darkness by His blood; have access into the Holiest of all through the blood; and live in protection by His blood. Let us partake of Christ, our Passover Lamb, and live under the protection and power of His blood.

9

The Protective Ministry of Angels

"For he shall give his angels charge over thee, to keep thee in all thy ways. They shall bear thee up in their hands, lest thou dash thy foot against a stone" (Ps. 91:11-12).

God has conferred upon His angels the responsibility of ministering or serving those whom He has ordained to be heirs of salvation. The writer of Hebrews confidently exclaims in chapter 1:14,

"But to which of the angels said he at any time, Sit on my right hand, until I make thine enemies thy foot stool? Are they not all ministering spirits, sent forth to minister for them who shall be heirs of salvation?

Angels are created heavenly beings, called in the Hebrew, "malak" and in the Greek, "angelos", both meaning "messenger" or "angel". These terms in the Old and New Testaments are used to refer to heavenly beings (Ps. 104:4; Gen. 32:1; Lk. 2:9, 15) or humans (Gen. 32:3; Mal. 2:7; Rev. 1:20) depending on the literary context.

These supernatural beings, called angels, are assigned by God to minister to His people – the heirs of salvation. The object of their ministry is the heirs of salvation. Salvation is from the Greek rendering: "soteria", and it is used in Scripture to denote material and temporal deliverance from human enemies (Lk. 1:69, 71; Acts 7:25; physical health (Acts 27:34); deliverance from the flood (Heb. 11:7); and any other evil known to mankind (Ps. 91:10, 16). Moreover, salvation also signifies spiritual and eternal deliverance for those who have received Christ Jesus as their personal Saviour (Acts 4:12; Rom. 10:9-10); deliverance from the bondage of sin (Phil. 2:12) and all the eternal consequences that accompany it (Rom. 5:9).

Angels aid in bringing about the deliverance of men and women in the earth whether eternal or temporal. They deliver and preserve the life of those who have inherited and shall inherit salvation. Throughout the Bible, you see that angels are involved in securing the fulfilment of God's purposes in the lives of God's people.

There are angels who function as mediators of special revelation (Zech. 1:9; Dan. 9:21-22); they give skill, understanding and interpretation of visions and dreams. Another function of angelic ministry is for those angels who are specifically assigned for battle and military warfare – heavenly warriors – who fight against the enemies of God's people, whether natural or spiritual. Two angels are mentioned in Scripture, by name: Gabriel and Michael. The former is an agent of special revelation from God to man; the latter, a military agent of warfare (Dan. 9:20-23; Lk. 1:11-20; Dan. 10:13; Rev. 12:7). Both of these angelic functions have been used by God, in Scripture, to deliver, protect and preserve His people from evil. For example, an angel of God appeared to

Joseph, in a dream, warning him to take his wife, Mary, and her child, Jesus, and flee into Egypt because Herod sought to kill the young child, supposing to secure his throne (Matt. 2:13-14). This angel imparted a word of wisdom: a divine insight into a future event, coupled with an exhortation to flee into Egypt, thus averting danger. The angel said,

"...Arise, and take the young child and his mother, and flee into Egypt; and be thou there until I bring thee word: for Herod will seek the young child to destroy him" (Matt. 2:13b).

This word given to Joseph by the angel was a word of wisdom listed as one of the nine gifts of the Spirit (1 Cor. 12:8). It gave Joseph supernatural insight into the evil plots that was about to bear fruit – the murder of many children in Bethlehem "and all the coasts thereof" (Matt. 2:16). Joseph was given vital information before the murderous event took place for the angel said, "...Herod WILL SEEK the young child to destroy Him (Matt. 2:13). Similarly, God will dispatch His angels of revelation to warn us of impending danger and will give us instructions as to what to do. They will work in conjunction with the guidance of the Holy Spirit in our lives. For instance, an angel of the Lord spoke to Philip to go south in the way that leads from Jerusalem to Gaza (Acts 8:26). When he obeyed the voice of the angel, he saw an Ethiopian eunuch, sitting in his chariot, reading the scroll of Isaiah; then the Holy Spirit spoke to Philip to go near the chariot (v 29). There is always a harmony between the Holy Spirit and ministry of angels.

Now the archangel, Michael, and his angelic host are angels of war who fight battles on behalf of the saints of the Most High. In the latter days, the Bible warns:

"And at that time shall Michael stand up, the great prince which standeth for the children of thy people: and there shall be a time of trouble, such as never was since there was a nation even to that same time: and at that time thy people shall be delivered, every one that shall be found written in the book" (Dan. 12:1)

In the last days, Michael, the archangel, will stand to protect and deliver the Jewish remnant who are the children of Abraham according to the election of grace (Rom. 11:5-7). They are said to be written in the book of life – the Lamb's book of life (Rev. 13:8; 20:12, 15). In the time of Jacob's trouble in the period called the "great tribulation" (Matt. 24:15-21), Michael the great prince will stand for the remnant of Israel.

There are other assignments that angels have been charged with to aid the salvation of God's people such as angels who are assigned with the ministry of healing to the sick. In St John chapter 5, there was a pool called Bethesda where a multitude of sick and infirmed people lay, waiting for the stirring of the water. It then went on to state,

"For an angel went down at a certain season into the pool, and troubled the water: whosoever then first after the troubling of the water stepped in was made whole of whatsoever disease he had" (Jn. 5:4).

Here, we can see that an angel was sent by God, at a specific season, to trouble the water so that whoever first went down into the water was healed of whatever infirmity he had. This a scriptural example of angels being involved in the healing of the sick.

People have testified of God opening their eyes to see angels coming with new organs to replace the organs that were diseased such as hearts and kidneys, or even replace organs that were removed through surgery. Obviously, God gets the glory and praise, not angels, for He is the Creator of new organs. However, God does minister healing through angelic instrumentality. Also, in conjunction, angels are assigned to prevent plagues and diseases from coming to you. The previous verse and opening scripture to this chapter announces,

""There shall no evil befall thee, neither shall any plague come nigh thy dwelling. For he shall give his angels charge over thee to keep in all thy ways" (Ps. 91:10-11).

Notice that two verses: 10 and 11, are related by the conjunction "for". In other words, no evil occurrence will affect you, nor will any plague or diseases come near you because God shall give his angels the responsibility of guarding and keeping watch over you to keep you. This is what the verses are actually saying. Through the ministry of angels, sicknesses, diseases and plagues will be kept at bay.

There was a member of my local church who gave a testimony to me personally of her experience of being protected by angels. It was during winter and there was a substantial snow fall with freezing temperatures that made the roads icy and treacherous. She, her husband and family drove in their vehicle to the city centre. She parked the car and went shopping at the Bull Ring with her husband and two boys, even though many vehicles were left abandoned due to adverse conditions. When they returned to the car, her husband started the engine to drive off but the vehicle was not moving because of the slippery incline of the road. As they pondered what they were going to do, two young men came from nowhere and pushed the car up the incline. When she and her family turned around to give a gesture of goodbye and thanks, the men were nowhere to be seen. They had disappeared. God sent His angels to rescue them. Consequently, they were able to drive home.

Another function of the ministry of angels is that the God sends them in the miraculous provision of food and drink for His people in time of dire need and lack. God made miraculous provision of food and water for the children of Israel during their forty years of wilderness wandering. He rained manna from heaven and brought forth water out of the rock (Ex. 16:4, 7, 12-17; 17:1-6). The Bible tells us that angels were involved in the miraculous provision of bread from heaven, which the Israelites called manna. In Psalm 78:23-25, it states,

"Though he had commanded the clouds from above, and opened the doors of heaven, And had rained down manna upon them to eat, and had given them of the corn of heaven. Man did eat angels' food: he sent them meat to the full."

Here the psalmist recounts the years of Israel's wilderness wandering and states that God commanded the clouds above to rain down manna, the grain of heaven, for them to eat. He then calls it "angels' food". Why was it called angels' food? Was it that angels ate of this manna? No! Angels do not need food to survive, for they are immortal and live in a higher state of existence (Ps. 8:4-5; Heb. 2:6-7). There is a more reasonable and biblical explanation than this. God used angels in the miraculous provision of manna, that is why it was called "angels' food" (Ps. 78:25).

God's intervention through angels to meet our needs cannot be hindered by the dire circumstances or economic recession. As the Apostle Paul correctly said,

"My God shall supply all your need according to his riches in glory by Christ Jesus" (Phil. 4:19).

God is our Source, and He will meet our needs through whatever means He chooses, and one of those ways is by the ministry of angels. The Lord's wealth is not contingent upon the economic systems of this world for His kingdom rules over all. As the economic systems of this world get progressively worse, God's angels of provision will be dispatched to meet the financial needs of God's children irrespective of the famine or dire economic conditions.

Elijah fled into the wilderness from the deadly threat of Jezebel and fell asleep under a juniper tree. An angel awoke him and he saw a cake baked on coals and a cruse of water at his head (1 Kgs. 19:1-8). This reminds me of a true story where a mother was believing God for food so that she and her children would eat. Not too long after, she heard a thump at the threshold of the door. When she opened the door, there was food left at her door, and yet she saw no one. I believe God's angel had left food at her door. There are other similar stories of angelic provision.

Angels were involved in the life and ministry of Jesus. An angel protected Him from the sword of Herod (Matt. 2:13-14). Angels ministered to Jesus after His temptation in the wilderness (Matt. 4:11). An angel was dispatched to strengthen Jesus as He agonised in the garden of Gethsemane over His imminent crucifixion and death (Lk. 22:43-44). An angel rolled away the stone from the sepulchre at Christ's resurrection (Matt. 28:1-4). At the ascension of Christ, two angels appeared in white apparel, announcing to His disciples His definite return "in like manner" (Acts 1:9-11).

If angels were involved in the life and ministry of the Son of God, they will also be involved in the lives of born again believers (Heb. 1: 13-14). According to Psalm 91:11, angels are commissioned to keep us – to protect us – in all our ways: those ways in which we acknowledge Him as our Lord and Counsellor. The Bible states,

"Trust in the Lord with all thine heart; and lean not unto thine own understanding. In all thy ways acknowledge him, and he shall direct thy paths" (Prov. 3:5-6).

To have God's protective angels at all times, the passage of scripture points out three things do: 1) trust in the Lord wholeheartedly and without reservation; 2) lean not or trust not in your own understanding; and 3) consult him on every aspect of your life and give him the glory; then, he shall direct your paths either directly or through the ministry of angels.

Now, I want to show you how to activate the ministry of angels to serve and protect you in accordance with the written Word. There are also things that we should not do when trying to access the ministry of angels in their assignments from God. Firstly, the Word of God does not exhort us to worship or pray to angels. The Bible tells us that when the Apostle John had seen all the wonderful things that the angel showed him, he fell down to worship at the feet of the angel. But the angel responded by saying,

"...See thou do it not: for I am thy fellow servant, and of thy brethren the prophets, and of them which keep the sayings of this book: worship God" (Rev. 22:9).

The angel's response to John's angelic worship was that he should not do it, but to worship God only. Holy angels of God will not accept worship from anyone; they will only point you to the One who is worthy of all worship (see also Rev. 19:10). Angels of God are passionate about worshipping God and the Lamb of God Who are seated on the throne (Rev. 4-5).

The Apostle Paul admonishes us,

"let no man beguile you of your reward in a voluntary humility and WORSHIPPING OF ANGELS,..." (Col. 2:18a).

The Apostle Paul identifies the worshipping of angels to be after the commandments of men, and is not according to sound doctrine. It is driven by the spirit of deception. Secondly, we are not to pray to angels; we are instructed to pray to the Father in the Name of Jesus (Matt. 6:9; Lk. 11:1-2; Jn. 15:16; 16:23-24). Jesus was betrayed by Judas who came with a band of men, from the chief priest and elders, bearing swords and staves to arrest Him. Peter attacked a servant of the high priest and cut off his ear. Then Jesus instructed Peter to put back his sword in its place and then said,

"Thinkest thou that I cannot now pray to my Father, and he shall presently give me more than twelve legions of angels? But how then shall the scriptures be fulfilled, that thus it must be?" (Matt. 26:53-54).

Jesus shows here how He could invoke the protective ministry of angels against those who had come to arrest Him. Jesus said that He could release the ministry of angels by praying to His Father. Notice! It did not say he could pray to angels, but to His Father only. However, He laid aside this right and promise of protection to fulfil the scriptures by becoming a suffering Saviour for the redemption of mankind. By example, we are to pray to the Father and He will dispatch His angels on our behalf.

Another way of releasing the ministry of angels is through our powerful confession of the Word of God. Psalm 103:20 exhorts,

"Bless the LORD, ye his saints, that excel in strength, that do his commandments, hearkening unto the voice of his word."

This verse tells us that the angels of God listen to and act on the voice of God's Word. There are two things that allude to this statement: 1) the direct voice of God (Ps. 103:20); 2) the voicing of God's Word back to Him by the believer (Ps. 119:49; Eph. 6:17). I will now deal with the latter as it concerns the Christian believers.

God has given us the most powerful weapon in all the universe that releases angelic forces to minister on our behalf. That weapon is the Word of God. It is described as a two-edged sword that cuts both ways (Heb. 4:12). Therefore, it is of paramount importance that every believer engages with the Word in study and meditation so that the Word gets into their spirit and it becomes an essential part of their being and spiritual equipment (Prov. 4:20-22; Jn. 15:7).

When the Word of God is in your spirit, as you speak forth its words, life and power will usher out of your mouth and the angels that have already been assigned by God to you, will act on your behalf. The Word will not work while it remains within the pages of your Bible; you must give voice to God's Word whether speaking it to yourself or to God. The scripture tells us that the angels will respond as you voice the Word of God from its pages through your mouth. It is the strategy for building God's Word into your spirit (Josh. 1:8) so that the Word proceeding from your mouth will have the same authority and power as if God Himself had spoken it.

We have been given the sword of the Spirit which is the Word of God. The Greek term here for "word" is "rhema", denoting that which is spoken or uttered and related to an individual passage or verse of scripture that the Holy Spirit brings to your remembrance, in contrast to another Greek term for word: "logos", which connotes the whole body of truth, the reasoned word, the expression of a thought or concept (Vine 1985), the comprehension and understanding of something.

As victorious believers, let us possess the logos and rhema of scripture: the Word of God dwelling richly in all wisdom and spiritual understanding (Col. 3:16), and continually speaking God's Word out of your mouth (Josh. 1:8), and God's angels will always be there to bear you up in time of need. Jesus confronted the Devil in His hour of temptation and overcame him with the Word of God in His mouth (Matt. 4), and after His temptation, angels were dispatched to minister to Him (Matt. 4:11).

10

The Dominion of the Believer

"Thou shalt tread upon the lion and adder: the young lion and dragon shalt thou trample under feet. Because he hath set his love upon me, therefore will I deliver him: I will set him on high, because he hath known my name" (Ps. 91:13-14).

In the beginning of creation, dominion is what God created the man and his wife to walk in. They were delegated authority over the earth and over every living thing that moved upon the face of the earth. Their dominion was to be exercised under the rule of God as a Vice-regent. There are two significant things that need to be identified: 1) the origin of man's authority, and 2) His jurisdiction. These two aspects describe the whole concept of dominion.

According to Collins Dictionary, dominion is defined as rule and authority which also includes the land, sphere or area of influence or control, governed by a ruler or government. Jurisdiction is the right or power to administer justice or the extent of such right or power. Our authority and the extent of its use can be traced back to the beginning of creation:

"And God said, Let us make man in our image, after our likeness: and let them have dominion over the fish of the sea, and over the fowl of the air, and over the cattle, and over all the earth, and over every creeping thing that creepeth upon the earth...And God blessed them, and God said unto them, Be fruitful, and multiply, and replenish the earth, and subdue it: and have dominion over the fish of the sea, and over the fowl of the air, and over every living thing that moveth upon the earth" (Gen. 1:26, 28).

As man created in God's image and likeness, in righteousness and true holiness: an aspect of that image included man reflecting God's authority and dominion over the earth. The Bible states,

"The heaven, even the heavens, are the LORD's: but the earth hath he given to the children of men" (Ps. 115:16).

God bears direct rule in the heavens, but He gave authority to man to rule over the earth: all living organisms on land and in the sea, all vegetation and inanimate objects. As long as man exercised his dominion under God's authority, natural creation was at peace and harmony with man and each other. Staying under God's authority required obedience to His perfect will not to eat of the tree of knowledge of good and evil (Gen. 2:17). Man's harmony with God maintained harmony with the very things that were under his authority.

However, sin entered the world and death by sin (Gen. 3; Rom. 5:12-21). By sin, man gave up his authority to Satan to use and manipulate it against him and his posterity. Since the image of God in man was marred by sin, his dominion was also affected because his image and dominion are related. Now Satan had power to steal, kill and destroy; to bring war, hostility, hatred, destruction and disharmony into the earth. Nevertheless, God gave a promise of redemption that the Seed of the woman would come and crush the head of the serpent (Satan) and he would bruise His heel (Gen. 3:15). The head of the serpent signifies authority, therefore the woman's Seed will destroy the serpent's authority. In so doing, Satan will bruise His heel, denoting His minor sufferings and death (Is. 53). Through Christ's bruising at the Cross of Calvary by Satan, He paralysed the Devil and his authority over death (Heb. 2:13-15; Col. 2:15). And after Jesus was raised from the dead, He said to His disciples, which would include all His disciples throughout the ages,

"...All power (authority) is given unto me in heaven and in earth. Go ye therefore and teach (Gk make disciples of) all nations..." (Matt. 28:18-19a).

In Mark's account of the Great Commission, Jesus, the One possessing all authority in heaven and earth says,

"...Go ye into all the world and preach the gospel to every creature"
(Mk. 16:15).

Jesus Christ, invested with all authority in heaven and earth conferred that authority to His Church - authority in earth to carry out the Great Commission to preach the Gospel, to teach Christ's disciples and to perform supernatural signs in order to win the lost for Christ and to do Kingdom business on the earth.

The Dominion of the Believer

At this present time, the extent of the Church's acting authority is on earth.

The other aspect of the Church's authority is in heaven for we are seated with Christ in heavenly places (Eph. 1:20-23; 2:6-7). This authority will not be activated until Christ returns and we are changed from mortality to immortality (1 Thess. 4:16-18; 1 Cor. 15:50-55). Then, the saints in Christ will judge the world and exercise authority over angels (1 Cor. 6:2-3). But that authority is not to be exercised for now, it is for the ages to come as declared by the apostle Paul (Eph. 2:6-7).

At this time, the Church is appointed to exercise authority on earth regarding kingdom matters, issues pertaining to the earthly realm such as preaching the Gospel to save the lost, teaching the Word for discipleship development, casting out devils and healing the sick, promoting righteousness and holiness, shining as lights in a dark world (Phil. 2:15). Authority has been delegated to the Church in the Name of Jesus to enforce the victory that Jesus Christ obtained for us by proclaiming the Kingdom of God and performing its supernatural signs on earth (Matt. 10:1, 7-8). Jesus said,

> "And these signs shall follow them that believe; In my name shall they cast out devils; they shall speak with new tongues; They shall take up serpents; and if they drink any deadly thing, it shall not hurt them; they shall lay hands on the sick, and they shall recover" (Mk. 16:17-18).

Because Jesus was going back to heaven to take up His position of authority at the right hand of God, He conferred His authority to His disciples through His Name to act in His absence – to do the things that He would if He was physically present. This is known as the power of attorney. It is having the authority and supernatural ability to do the things that Jesus did. Therefore He made a profound statement to His disciples, just prior to His suffering and death, saying,

"Verily, verily, I say unto you, he that believeth on me, the works that I do shall he do also; and greater works than these shall he do; because I go unto my Father. And whatsoever ye shall ask in my name, that will I do, that the Father may be glorified in the Son" (Jn. 14:12-13).

Jesus preface His statement with a double annunciation: "Verily, verily," meaning truly, truly, because He was preparing them to receive a very profound truth about what they will be able to do in His Name. Among the works which Jesus did were, healing the sick, raising the dead, and casting out demons. Jesus shows us that faith is the key that unlocks your authority to do the works of Jesus and to do greater than these.

The following verses show us how these things will be done by the believer - by prayer in the authority of the Name of Jesus (v13, 14):

In Psalm 91:13-14, the Christian who knows who he is in Christ "will tread upon the lion and adder, the young lion and the dragon shall he trample under feet". Something that you trample under feet is an expression of dominion. The prerequisite to exercising dominion is stated in verse 14: "...because he hath known my name." I will write more on this later.

Possessing authority over the lion and serpent has a twofold meaning. What is true in the natural has its true counterpart in the realm of the Spirit, thus, the passage has both a natural and a spiritual connotation (Gen. 3:15). Regarding the natural, the Christian has been given dominion over the animal and reptilian kingdom.

In the Old Testament, there are examples of men of faith, who through the anointing of God, demonstrated their dominion over fierce and dangerous beasts. Samson of the tribe of Dan, a judge of Israel, had extraordinary and supernatural strength. The Bible tells us that when he came down to the vineyards of Timnath, a young lion roared against him; the Spirit of the LORD came mightily upon Samson and he tore the lion as he would have torn a kid (Judg. 14:5-6). The young lion was no match for the anointing – the Spirit of God – that was upon Samson. The Spirit of the LORD was the conveyor of divine authority and power that gave Samuel dominion over the young lion.

David, the son of Jesse, whom Samuel anointed to be the next king of Israel stated before king Saul, just prior to confronting the giant, Goliath of Gath, how that when a lion and a bear took a lamb from his father's flock, he pursued after him and delivered the lamb out of his mouth. When Goliath rose up against David, he held him by the beard and slew him (1 Sam. 17:33-35). David, a man of faith, was able to slay the lion and the bear because the authority and power of God was upon him; he is also listed in Faith's Hall of Fame (Heb. 11:32-33).

Daniel, a man with an excellent spirit, was a captive of the children of Judah in Babylon whom God had promoted under the reign of Darius, King of Persia who sought to exalt him over his whole realm (Dan. 6:1-3). But there were certain princes and presidents who were seeking an occasion to find fault with which to accuse him before the king, but they found nothing (v4, 5). So they tricked the king in signing a decree forbidding any man to petition any god or man for thirty days. Inspite of this law, Daniel continued to pray to the God of Israel. As a result, Daniel was charged and thrown into a den of lions. While he was in the lion's den, God dispatched an angel to shut the lion's mouths so that no harm came to Daniel. He was given dominion over the lions and was delivered (Dan. 6).

In the New Testament, Jesus conferred authority upon His disciples to tread on serpents and scorpions, even to pick them up without being overpowered by them (Lk. 10:19; Mk. 16:18). I have already mentioned how a venomous serpent fastened itself to the Apostle Paul's hand and he, shaking it off into the fire, felt no harm (Acts 28:3-6).

Not only can we exercise dominion in the realm of the natural, but we can also demonstrate authority in the realm of the spirit. Jesus said,

"Behold, I give unto you power [Gk authority] to tread on serpents and scorpions, and over all the power [Gk ability] of the enemy: and nothing shall by any means hurt you" (Lk. 10:19).

Jesus gave His disciples all authority: that is over all the power and ability of the enemy. That authority is absolute. There is no power of the enemy that can resist the absolute authority given to Jesus' disciples. Jesus made the above statement after the seventy disciples returned from their mission stating that the devils were subject unto them through His Name (v17). How were they subject to their authority? They commanded the devils to come out of the oppressed and they obeyed. This is how we tread upon serpents and scorpions, lions and dragons (Ps. 91:13; Lk. 10:19).

Satan is described in Scripture as a lion who walks about, seeking whom he may devour; who must be resisted with the authority Christ has given us (1 Peter 5:8-9; Jam. 4:7). He is also identified as a dragon – the old serpent that deceives the whole world (Rev. 12:9). Not only do we have authority over the lion, that is, Satan's power to hurt and destroy, but we also have dominion over the serpent or dragon, which are the Devil's deceptions, lies and cunning devices. In Scripture, the lion is the symbol of strength and power (Judg. 14:8-9, 12-18); the serpent is the symbol of lies and deceptions (Gen. 3:1-6; 2 Cor. 11:3). Yet! God has given us dominion over both.

The Apostle Paul demonstrated his authority over serpents both in the natural and in the realm of the spirit. In Philippi, Paul was confronted by a young girl who had a spirit of divination. She brought much financial gain to her masters by soothsaying. She followed Paul, Silas and Luke for many days exclaiming that they were servants of the Most High God which show us the way of salvation. But Paul being grieved in his spirit, discerning that it was an unclean spirit speaking through her, commanded the unclean spirit to come out of her, and it came out the same hour (Acts 16:16-18).

This spirit of divination is described in the Greek language as a spirit of puthon (Acts 16:16). Puthon is the Greek term from which the English word "python" is derived. In Greek mythology, it referred to a Pythian serpent or dragon dwelling in Pytho, at the bottom of mount Parnassus, guarding the oracle of Delphi (Vine 1985), hence, the Greek word puthon is translated divination in the King James Bible.

The Apostle Paul exercised authority over this serpent spirit that was in the young girl, and cast it out in the Name of Jesus Christ (Acts 16:18). Having authority over demons protects you from their ability to hurt and harm you. That is why Jesus concludes His statement in Luke 10:19 with, "...and nothing shall by any means hurt you."

There are two important keys, in Psalm 91:14, which will unlock the consciousness of our dominion in Christ. The verse states,

"Because he hath set his love upon me, therefore will I deliver him: I will set him on high, because he hath known my name.

This verse is a transition from the psalmist speaking to God, in response to the psalmist's confession. God mentions two things that He desires His people to earnestly seek after: 1) to set their love upon Him; 2) to know His Name – that is to know Him.
Loving God is to be passionate about Him. Jesus declared this as the most important commandment of all (Matt. 22:36-38). This command of love will bring about the fulfilment of all commandments (v39-40; Rom. 13:8-10). And on the basis of this great commandment, the Lord said that He would deliver you; and so the Lord will deliver you from the power of Satan whose dominion feeds and thrives on the fear of others (Heb. 2:14-15). But thanks be to God for His perfect love that counteracts fear. That perfect love in us will give us boldness against the enemy because perfect love expels all fear (1 Jn. 4:17-19).

The second requirement to walking in dominion is to know His Name. Names were considered very important in the religion and culture of the patriarchs and nation of Israel. Names signified a person: their character, authority, work or ministry, and was often prophetic, speaking of some future purpose or event as well as a previous or present experience.

In the genealogy of Adam, Enoch, who prophesied of the second coming of the Lord (Jude 1:14), called his own son Methuselah, which meant "his death shall bring forth" (Gen. 5:21-22). If you calculate the years from Methuselah's birth up to his death, it will add up to nine hundred and sixty-nine years and you will discover that Methuselah had died in the year of the flood. In other words, Noah's flood did not come until Methuselah died; hence his death brought forth the flood. His name was prophetic.

Noah's name was prophetic because his father Lamech, stated that his son would comfort them concerning their work and toil of their hands. Therefore his name means comfort. Noah's destiny would bring about the removal of the curse of the ground after the flood (Gen. 5:28-29; 8:20-21).

Abram's name meaning "exalted father", was changed to Abraham which also meant "father of a multitude" because God declared that He had made him a father of many nations (Gen. 17:4-5; Rom. 4:17). His new name was not only prophetic but it also depicted who he now was – his person, character and position in the Kingdom of God. Abraham embraced the promise of who he was and therefore would become as a result of Christ's redemptive work (Gal. 3:13-14, 26-29).

God made Himself known to Moses and Israel by the Name, Yahweh, and it depicts His Self-existence, the eternalness and the immutability of His character. It indicates that as Yahweh, He had come to demonstrate His faithfulness to the promise He made to Abraham, Isaac and Jacob in delivering His people from Egyptian bondage unto the Promised Land, Canaan. His mighty acts were revelations of His Name and if they sought to know Him and obey Him, He promised to set them on high above all the nations of the earth (Deut. 28:1).

In the New Testament, the God of Israel robed Himself in flesh (Jn. 1:14; 1 Tim. 3:16) and was given the Name Jesus, which described the work He had come to do – save His people from their sins (Matt. 1:21; Lk. 2:21). All the Old Testament Names of God have their fulfilment in the Name of Jesus. He completed His work of redemption on the Cross, arose from the dead and has been exalted to the right hand of God, having been given all authority in heaven and earth (Matt. 28:18).

Jesus, a man with all authority, has delegated His authority to His Church. This has a threefold meaning: 1) It signifies our union with Him in the likeness of His death, burial, resurrection (Rom. 6:1-6) and ascension to the right hand of God (Eph. 1:20-22; 2:5-6); 2) His Name conveys the fact that we are now functioning on the earth in His stead (2 Cor. 5:20); 3) in His Name, we have been delegated with His authority to do the work of the Kingdom (Lk. 10:17-19; Mk. 16:15-18).

Let us rise up to the consciousness of who we are in Christ and begin to exercise our dominion over the works and forces of darkness and utilise the victory that Jesus obtained for us at the Cross of Calvary (Col. 2:14-15).

11

The Sevenfold Will of God

"Because he hath set his love upon me, therefore will I deliver him: I will set him on high, because he hath known my name. He shall call upon me, and I will answer him: I will be with him in trouble; I will deliver him, and honour him. With long life will I satisfy him, and shew him my salvation" (Ps. 91:14-16).

From Psalm 91:1-13, the psalmist makes his positive confessions about the God of Israel being his Protector, and then from verse 14-16, God speaks confirming His promise of deliverance and protection for those who put their trust in Him. Thus, God's Will is stated and affirmed to the psalmist.

There are seven specific promises pronounced by God concerning those who will abide in that secret place. I have entitled these seven promises as the sevenfold Will of God because the context of these promises are prefaced with "I will", hence the title of this chapter: "The Sevenfold Will of God".

In Biblical numerology, the number seven is symbolic of perfection, completion, fullness and rest. For example, God created the heavens and the earth in six days and rested on the seventh because he had finished His creation (Gen. 2:1-3).

The sevenfold manifestation of the Holy Spirit upon Messiah depicted the perfection of His character (Rev. 5:6), the fullness of His Spirit (Jn. 3:34), the anointing of Jesus to give rest to the weary and fainthearted (Matt. 3:11; 11:28-29; Is. 28:11-12; 1ˆsCor.14:2
). There are other examples such as the seven stars and the seven golden candlesticks which are the seven angels of the seven churches (Rev. 1:20).

The seven promises of Psalm 91:14-16 depicts the perfect Will of God (Rom. 12:2) that brings you into His fullness, His rest and His completeness.

The following promises listed are these:

1. Deliverance: "...therefore will I deliver him..." (v14a)
2. Exaltation: "...I will set him on high..." (v14)b
3. Answered Prayer: "He shall call upon me, and I will answer him" (v15a)
4. God's Abiding Presence in turbulent times: "...I will be with him in trouble..." (v15b)
5. Honour: "...I will...honour him" (v15)
6. Satisfaction With Long Life: "With long life will I satisfy him..." (v16a)
7. Salvation: "...and shew him my salvation" (16b).

Deliverance

To "deliver" comes from the Hebrew word "palat", meaning to escape, save or deliver. In verse 14, God is the subject of this verb; He is the initiator of our deliverance and will cause us to escape evil in a time of temptation, as mentioned in the Lord's Prayer (Matt. 6:13). Temptation is at the very root of spiritual warfare and applying the principles already mentioned in this book will cause you to escape the plots and cunning devices the enemy has set in your way to ensnare you. But God has promised that He will deliver you from the snare of the fowler (Ps. 91:3). The Word of God tells us that God is faithful Who will not permit us to be tempted above that which you are able to bear, but He will, in the temptation, make a way of escape that you may be able to bear it (1 Cor. 10:13); and that includes any adverse situation you come across in life. We are already more than conquerors through him that loved us (Rom. 8:37).

Exaltation

When you are delivered, you are promoted in the realm of the Spirit. Adversities and afflictions are launching pads for promotion. Each time God delivers, you are elevated from one level of glory to another. This is how the Kingdom of God works. For example, Shadrach, Meshech, Abednego and Daniel faced

God promises in Psalm 91:15 that if you call upon Him, He will answer you. The purpose of prayer is to get an answer, or else why are you praying? Everyone who prays, petitions God with the intention of getting an answer. That answer, based on faith on God's Word and promises, is never yes or no; it is always yes (1 Jn. 5:14-15; 2 Cor. 1:20)!

The New Testament assures us that God's heart is to answer our prayers of faith by giving us the very things we have asked for. Jesus declares to us in His teachings, God's desire to answer every petition made by His children:

"Ask, and it shall be given you; seek, and you shall find; knock, and it shall be opened unto you: For every one that asketh receiveth; and he that seeketh findeth; and to him that knocketh it shall be opened" (Matt. 7:7-8).

God is not partial concerning His children; this promise is for every child of God who comes to Him in faith (Acts 10:35). Jesus clearly stated, "For EVERY ONE that asketh receiveth..." (v8). God's will is that every one who asks, receives. This reveals two important elements to effectual prayer: 1) asking; 2) receiving. Many are good at doing the first but not the latter. It is so easy to ask without receiving; this is what I call a religious prayer – praying without expectation.
Jesus, in another passage, teaches on how to ask and receive when praying, in Mark 11:24,

"Therefore I say unto you, What things soever ye desire [Gk ask], when ye pray, believe that ye receive them, and ye shall have them."

You receive by believing that you already have received what you have asked for based on God's Word, regardless of how you feel or what you see the circumstances are dictating. Base your prayers on the promises of God's Word which are yes and amen (2 Cor. 1:20). The specific word that God has given us is this: "He shall call upon me, and I will answer him..."

God's Abiding Presence in Turbulent Times

God says, "...I will be with him in trouble..." (Ps. 91:15b). The issue here is not whether God will be with you in trouble, for He has said and cannot lie (Num. 23:19; Heb. 6:18). What we need to focus on is developing a consciousness of God's Presence to the point that it becomes more real than the adverse circumstances you are going through.

In many passages of scripture, God declares that He will never leave us nor forsake us. Prior to Jesus' ascension to the right hand of God, he announced to His disciples:

"...lo, I am with you always, even unto the end of the world. Amen" (Matt. 28:20b).

Jesus made a factual statement that He is with us always even until the end of the world and ratified His announcement with an "Amen", meaning so be it. You may ask, how is He always going to be with His disciples if He was about to ascend into heaven to be with His Father? Well, put it this way; Jesus in His physical bodily presence, as a man ascended to heaven while in

His invisible divine essence remained with them in the Person of the Holy Spirit.

Before Jesus' death and crucifixion, he promised them that He would send the Holy Spirit to abide with them for ever – to live on the inside of them (Jn. 14:16-17). Then He says, "I will not leave you comfortless [Gk orphans], I will come to you" (v18). According to the verse preceding this, it is made possible through the ministry and presence of the Holy Spirit. The Spirit abiding in us (v16-17) is the Father and the Son who have come to make their abode in us (v23).

The key to walking in victory is about developing a God-inside consciousness attitude, through meditating in the Word (Josh. 1:8; Ps. 1:2; Phil. 4:8-9); praise and worship (Ps. 22:3; 8:2; Eph. 5:18-19); and praying in tongues (1 Cor. 14:2, 14-15, 18; Eph. 6:18). These godly practices will strengthen and equip you to always have an awareness of God's Presence which will expel fear, weakness and despondency (Josh. 1:5, 9; Ps. 118:6).

Honour

God also said, "...I will...honour him" (Ps. 91:15c). The word "honour" is translated from the Hebrew rendering "kabed", which basically means to be heavy or weighty. Its biblical usage connotes, to be "grievous, hard, rich, honourable and glorious." This Hebrew root appears three hundred and seventy-six times in the Tenach – the Hebrew Scriptures. It is also the Hebrew root from which the word "kabod" is derived, meaning "glory".

"Kabed" is used both in a positive and negative sense, but for the sake of relevance, conciseness and specificity, I will expound on its positive aspects.

"Kabed" is used figuratively of a weighty person in the sense of being honourable, impressive, excellent, virtuous, worthy of respect and held in high esteem. This usage occurs in more than half of its appearances in the Old Testament (TWOT 1980:426 Vol. 1). It is descriptive of someone's reputation and character being honourable, honoured, glorious and glorified, of which includes a high social position and wealth (Gen. 13:2).

When God honours a person who honours Him, that honour will include recognition and greatness in the Kingdom of God (Matt. 11:11; 18:1-4); a royal position of authority (Eph. 2:6); great wealth and riches (2 Cor. 8:9; 9:8; Phil. 4:19; 3 Jn. 1:2) and His Life – righteousness and true holiness (2 Cor. 3:18; Eph. 4:24).

SATISFACTION WITH LONG LIFE

"With long life will I satisfy him..." God desires His people to live a long and fulfilled life. In Exodus 23:25-26 it states,

"And ye shall serve the LORD thy God, and he shall bless thy bread, and thy water; and I will take sickness away from the midst of thee. There shall nothing cast their young, nor be barren, in thy land: the number of thy days I will fulfil."

God fulfilling your days, denotes that your life or days will not be cut short because of some deadly sickness or disease; your days being fulfilled clearly describes God's deliverance and protection from the very things that will shorten your life. He said he will bless your bread and water; that is, when you give God thanks for the food and water He has provided, they will not harm or contaminate your life because you have acknowledged God as the Source of all good things (1 Tim. 4: 3-5; Mk. 16:18; Ja. 1:17).

He promised to take sickness away from the midst of you so that your life will be long and satisfied. In Psalm 91:16, He did not promise just to give you long life, no! He said that He would satisfy you with long life. There are many in society who have long life. In fact, people in Great Britain are living longer because of advancement in medical science, and yet their lives are not satisfied or fulfilled. Satisfaction with long life includes the length and quality of life.

Quality of life entails divine health and peace of mind; spiritual wellbeing and abundant blessings; fulfilment of God's Will for your life - having completed what you were born to do. There is no greater satisfaction than to complete your God-given assignment and to have the spiritual and physical wellbeing to do it. That is quality of life. Submission to God's authority including His direct and delegated authority will unlock the blessings of longevity and wellbeing according to Ephesians 6:2-3,

"Honour thy father and mother, which is the first commandment with promise; That it may be WELL WITH THEE, and thou mayest LIVE LONG on the earth."

SALVATION

"...and shew him my salvation" (Ps. 91:16b). The Hebrew concept of salvation entails two aspects: temporal and spiritual deliverance. Temporal deliverance means to be free from one's enemies, fear, disease, adversities and so on. Spiritual deliverance involves forgiveness of sins, deliverance from sin's power, and a future life that culminates in the Messianic Kingdom of God.

The term "salvation" in Psalm 91:16 is translated from the Hebrew word "yeshua", meaning deliverance or salvation. According to its context, it implies deliverance from all spiritual and temporal adversities listed in the chapter; it denotes freedom from all kinds of evil whether, moral, spiritual or temporal. The Hebrew word "yeshua", is a full package of benefits and blessings.

This Hebrew word "yeshua" is the Hebrew equivalent for Jesus in the Greek New Testament, also meaning deliverance or salvation. Jesus' Name according to the Hebrew usage speaks of total deliverance from all evil. There is no evil or adversity that is not covered by that Name. Jesus came to provide salvation for the whole man: spirit, soul and body (1 Thess. 5:23). His Name reflected His person, character, work and mission (Matt. 1:21; Acts 4:12). All the promises and benefits of deliverance listed in the whole chapter of Psalm 91 are packaged in that Name (2 Cor. 1:20).

When Greek-speaking Jews translated the Hebrew Old Testament into Greek, they used the Greek word "soterion" to convey the comprehensive idea of "yeshua". This very word was used by

Simeon to identify the baby Jesus when He was brought to the Temple to be dedicated (Lk. 2:30).

To appropriate this salvation, it comes in the same way that you begun – believing with the heart and confessing with the mouth. The Bible states,

"That if thou shall confess with thy mouth the Lord Jesus, and shalt believe in thine heart that God hath raised him from the dead, thou shalt be saved. For with the heart man believeth unto righteousness; and with the mouth confession is made unto salvation" (Rom. 10:9-10).

Every blessing in salvation, God says He wants to show it unto us – to have it manifested in our lives. To have something legally provided for us, will not do us any good unless we appropriate all these blessings to become experiential. Let us take advantage of the fullness of our salvation by faith and see the salvation of the Lord.

12

Persecution in the Light of God's Protection Policy

"yea, and all that will live godly in Christ Jesus shall suffer persecution" (2 Tim. 3:12).

Having concluded my discourse on Psalm 91, I thought it would be wise, in keeping with the correct principles of biblical interpretation, to address a side that is unfavourable to human nature – even to many Christians. I deem it important as a student and teacher of the Word of God to present any truth in the context of the whole Bible, for isolation will lead to error – a text out of context is a pretext.

Therefore, I want to present this book as a balanced approach to the subject of God's Protection Policy in the light of the fact that those who live godly shall suffer persecution. Does Psalm 91 promise us freedom from persecution? And if not, is God contradicting His promise of protection? How do we reconcile two seemingly contradictory truths when in reality they are both stated clearly to be part of the Christian life as declared in the opening verse of this chapter? I will attempt to answer this.

Our Lord Jesus Christ is the prime example and model for every Christian's manner of life, ministry and influence in the world. This spiritual axiom is conveyed by Jesus:

"The disciple is not above his master, not the servant above his lord. It is enough for the disciple that he be as his master, and the servant as his lord. If they have called the master of the house Beelzebub, how much more shall they call them of his household" (Matt. 10:24-25).

Jesus again reminded His disciples of these words the night of His betrayal:

"Remember the word that I said unto you, The servant is not greater than his lord. If they have persecuted me, they will also persecute you; if they have kept my saying, they will keep yours also" (Jn. 15:20).

These two passages convey the fact that Jesus is also an example of how the world would treat His disciples. If they persecuted Him, they will also persecute His followers; if they received Him, they will also receive His disciples. Why? Because the disciples are not above their Teacher nor servants above their Lord. The reality is that Jesus Christ was persecuted by the Jews; not everyone accepted Him (Jn. 1:10-11). The Bible states that the Jews persecuted Jesus for three reasons: because He broke their Sabbath tradition; claimed to be the Son of God thus making Himself equal with God; and as the Light of the world - men loved the darkness rather than the Light because their deeds are evil (Jn. 5:16-18; 3:19).

After Jesus' baptism in the River Jordan and temptation in the wilderness, He returned to His own town, Nazareth, entered the synagogue and began to read from the book of Isaiah (61:1-2) announcing His Messiahship and the fulfilment of scripture. The crowd were offended at Him, drew Him out of the town and led Him to the edge of the cliff intending to throw Him down; but He supernaturally passed through the midst of them and went His way. God's protection was upon Jesus in His time of persecution and was delivered out of their hands (Lk. 4:16-30; Jn. 8:58-59; 10:31-39).

There are several other biblical instances where God delivered His Son out the hands of His persecutors when they tried to arrest Him or kill Him. Jesus abode as a man in that Secret Place while ministering in Israel. John the Apostle in his narration of the life of Christ would repeatedly make a statement that accompanied God's protection of His Son from the hands of His persecutors. That statement is this: His hour was not yet come (Jn. 7:6, 30, 44; 8:20).

Approaching the time of His sufferings and death, He began to exclaim, "The hour is come" (Jn. 12:23) and refers to the hour of His sufferings (Jn. 12:27, 31-32; 13:1). He lays aside His divine rights of protection to fulfil God's redemptive purpose; that is why He said,

"...I lay down my life for the sheep...Therefore doth my Father love me, because I lay down my life, that I might take it again. No man take it from me, but I lay it down of myself. I have power [Gk authority] to lay it down, and I have power [Gk authority] to take it again. This commandment have I received of my Father"

(Jn. 10:15c, 17-18).

Since Jesus Christ lived under God's protection from His birth to His death, it was impossible for anyone to take His life from Him, no! He freely laid it down for us. A man who does not live in God's secret place of protection can have His life taken from him by human violence, sickness, disease, poverty and calamity, but the person who abides under the shadow of the Almighty is protected from all these things until he is ready to lay down His life only for the sake of the Gospel to fulfil some redemptive purpose. As Jesus Christ laid down His life for us, we ought also to lay down our life for the brethren (1 Jn. 3:16).

Jesus could have appropriated the protection benefit of having twelve legions of angels to come to His rescue, but forfeited this deliverance in order to do His Father's will and bring glory to His Name (Matt. 26:52-54; Jn. 12:23, 27-28). According to Hebrews 11, what is said about the elders of faith could also be said about our Lord and Saviour:

"...others were tortured, not accepting deliverance; that they might obtain a better resurrection" (v35).

Jesus Christ was tortured by scourging and crucifixion, not accepting deliverance that he might obtain a better resurrection. In laying down His life, He has authority to take it up again in His resurrection.

Suffering for the Christian life is not appealing to the flesh, nevertheless, it is a calling for the follower of Christ. In fact, here is the balance of the Christian calling; called to suffer for His Name sake (1 Peter 2:20-21), and called to inherit a blessing (1

Peter 3:9). This twofold calling is also reiterated by our Lord in His beatitudes:

""Blessed are they which are persecuted for righteousness' sake: for theirs is the kingdom of heaven. Blessed are ye when men shall revile you, and persecute you, and shall say all manner of evil against you falsely, for my sake. Rejoice and be exceeding glad: for great is your reward in heaven: for so persecuted they the prophets which were before you" (Matt. 5:10-12).

We are blessed in our sufferings when we are mistreated and falsely accused for the sake of Christ and His righteousness, for in this, God is glorified. Our calling is to be a partaker of Christ's sufferings (1 Peter 4:13). The Bible states,

"Forasmuch then as Christ hath suffered for us in the flesh, arm yourselves with the same mind: for he that hath suffered in the flesh hath ceased from sin; That he no longer should live the rest of his time in the flesh to the lusts of men, but to the will of God" (1 Peter 4:1-2).

There is a spiritual tension that exists between the Kingdom of God and the kingdom of this world because their norm and values are diametrically opposed to each other, so that those who belong to this worldly system will fight against those who belong to the heavenly Kingdom from above. Citizens of God's Kingdom who suffer are seeking to do the will of God against the lusts of the flesh. Conversely, those who seek only to fulfil their own lusts and desires contravene the will of God. Therefore anything that threatens their "freedom" to satisfy their own fleshly cravings will seek to eliminate it through persecution. Consequently, it is inevitable. This is the true nature of Christian suffering and persecution from a biblical perspective.

Those who "hate" their lives in this world have committed them under God's protection, therefore they will have the authority of laying down their lives, if need be, for the redemption and advancement of His Kingdom (Jn. 12:25b). On the other hand, those who love their own lives in this world will have it taken from them through sin, disease, natural disasters and calamities that come as a result of the curse of judgment of God because they are not under divine protection. These are not for the believer who has already laid his life down to follow Christ, and would, yet again, do so in death (Matt. 16:24-25).

Partaking of the sufferings of Christ does not include the things He came to carry away in His sacrificial death, so that we would be free (Is. 53; Matt. 8:16-17; 1 Peter 2:24). The things He carried away that were not to be a part of Christian sufferings were moral and spiritual weakness (1 Peter 2:19-21; 3:16-17; 4:15-16); sickness, disease and demonic torment (Is. 63:5; Matt. 8:16-17; 1 Peter 2:24); poverty and lack (Is. 53:5; Mk. 10:28-30; 2 Cor. 8:9; 9:8); accidents or violence instigated by men because of being in the wrong place at the wrong time; disastrous storms and weather patterns (Ps. 91).

The Apostle Paul was called by the revelation (vision) of Jesus Christ to be His disciple and apostle to the Gentiles after obtaining letters from the high priest to persecute and arrest men and women, who called upon the name of Jesus, and bring them to Jerusalem (Acts 8:1-8; 26:19; Gal. 1:11-12). Included in this calling was that he would suffer great things for the Name of Jesus (Acts 9:15-16). Paul worked more than the other apostles (1 Cor. 15:9-10) and also suffered more, describing it as a thorn in the flesh:

the angel of Satan to buffet him (2 Cor. 12:7). Paul declares that this thorn in the flesh was given him lest he should be exalted above measure through the abundance of revelations he received (v6-7). He prayed three times for it to be removed (v8), but the Lord responded,

"...My grace is sufficient for thee: for my strength is made perfect in weakness..."

Two things are said about the grace of God: it is sufficient and it has perfect strength in weakness. God's grace is sufficient because it is exceedingly abundant (Rom. 5:17, 20), and secondly, it is equated with strength. Grace is not merely the unmerited favour of God (Eph. 2:8-9) but is also the divine enablement: the strength and power to do what truth demands of us (2 Cor. 12:9; 2 Tim. 2:1; Jn. 1:16-17). The purpose of God's grace upon the Apostle Paul was to strengthen him spiritually, ethically and morally to endure the challenges and difficulties that he would face in preaching the Word.

Now what was the nature of those difficult challenges? Paul tells us in the next verse (v10),

"Therefore I take pleasure in infirmities, in reproaches, in necessities, in distresses for Christ's sake: for when I am weak, then I am strong."

The things listed in the above verse that Paul went through - the infirmities, reproaches, necessities and distresses, were sufferings for the sake of Christ and the expansion of His Kingdom. According to the immediate and whole context of the New Testament, his sufferings relates to persecution (Matt. 5:10-12). In the previous chapter, the apostle gives a detailed list of the things he suffered for the sake of Christ: in more abundant labours, stripes above measure, in prisons frequently, often exposed to death (v23), five times scourged by the Jews with thirty-nine stripes, three times beaten with rods, stoned once, suffered shipwreck three times, a night and a day in the sea, and the list goes on (see 2 Cor. 11:23-33).

Paul's use of the phrase "thorn in the flesh" is designated to describe the nature of his sufferings, applying the correct terminology in accordance with Old Testament theology. This term or similar terms were also used in the Old Testament that the Apostle Paul was aware of as a scholar and rabbi of the Scriptures (Judg. 2:3; Josh. 23:13; Nu. 33:55; Ezek. 28:24). These passages spoke of Israel's enemies being pricks in their eyes and thorns in their sides. In other words, they would be a distress, a nuisance and a snare to them – so vividly exemplified in the history of the book of Judges.

The terms, "thorn in the flesh" and "thorn in the side", were never used to denote sickness or disease; they were only used to refer to circumstances which caused persecution and oppression, such as the nations surrounding Israel, or the messenger of Satan that used human personalities to stir up persecution against Paul so that he would not be exalted above measure.

In the midst of all these trials God frequently delivered Paul from death (2 Cor. 4:8-12; 11:23-26; 2 Tim. 4:17-18). He would ask the brethren to pray for him to be delivered out of the hands of his persecutors (2 Thess. 3:1-2; Rom. 15:30-31; 2 Cor. 1:8-10). He continued to walk in God's supernatural protection from death as he ministered the Word. While his work was not complete,

God protected him. But there came a time that the apostle Paul was martyred for the Name of Jesus for the following principles:

1. Like Jesus, he finished the work that God gave him to do (1 Tim. 4:7; Jn. 17:4)
2. He was ready to be offered up for Christ (2 Tim. 4:6; Rev. 3:2)
3. He refused to be delivered that he may obtain a better resurrection (Heb. 11:35)
4. He knew that the time of his death was at hand (1 Tim. 4:6; 2 Peter 1:13-14)
5. His sufferings and death would serve a redemptive purpose for himself (Phil. 1:21, 23; 2 Cor. 5:8; Ja. 1:2-4) and for others (1 Jn. 3:16; 1 Peter 2:12)
6. Suffering for Jesus' sake glorifies God (Jn. 21:18-19; 1 Peter 1:6-8; 4:16).

Any suffering that is not for Christ or the furtherance of the Gospel does not glorify God. According to Psalm 91, we have been redeemed from sufferings that cause a person's life to deteriorate, eventually taking it. When we suffer for the Name of Christ, we are laying down our lives for Him. Living under God's protection, our lives cannot be taken from us.

For example, there two instances recorded in the book of Acts of stoning: Stephen (Acts 7:57-60), and Paul (Acts 14:19-20). Stephen, the first recorded martyr, testified against the Jews for their hardness of heart; they drew him out of the city and stoned him. It was not the stones that took his life but the petition he offered to the Lord: "Lord Jesus, receive my spirit" and praying for his persecutors, the Bible says "he fell asleep" (v60). He freely and willingly laid down his life for Christ. Jesus had made a similar petition to His Father when He laid down His life (Lk. 23:46).

The Apostle Paul, having preached the Gospel at Lystra, was stoned by the inhabitants of the city as a result of Jews going there to stir up the people. They threw him out of the city, supposing he was dead. However, certain disciples surrounded him and Paul rose up, went into the city and departed with Barnabas the next day, to Derbe. The Holy Spirit in Paul strengthened him that he rose up and departed the next day. This could only be the power of God.

After such a terrible stoning, you would think it would have taken several days to recover. But Paul had a revelation that the same Spirit that raised up Jesus from the dead would make alive his mortal body (Rom. 8:11). The Apostle did not die for the reasons stated previously: his work was not done; he was not ready to die. Therefore, refusing to give up his life in death, the Spirit strengthened him.

There are various kinds of persecution that Christians suffer for the sake of Christ, such as verbal abuse and false accusations (Matt. 5:11; 1 Peter 2:23); physical abuse: scourging, beatings, bonds, imprisonment, stoning, torture, the spoiling of one's possession including political, social or religious status, rejection and death (Heb. 11:36-38; Phil. 3:4-8; Is. 53:3).

Persecution is one of the signs Jesus spoke of that we are experiencing in the end times:

"Then shall they deliver you up to be afflicted, and shall kill you: and ye shall be hated of all nations for my name's sake. And then shall many be offended, and shall betray one another, and shall hate one another...And because iniquity shall abound, the love of many shall wax cold. But he that shall endure unto the end, the same shall be saved" (Matt. 24:9-10, 12-13).

God's people are suffering persecution around the world, especially in Islamic and communist countries. We must always remember to pray for them and the work of God in those countries, that the Word of God may have free course; praying that God will grant them supernatural protection to spread the Gospel.

Whether we live or die, we are more than conquerors through him who loved us, for no persecution or death can overcome us nor separate us from God's love (Rom. 8:35-39). According to the Olivet discourse (Matt. 24), God's people will be afflicted, hated and even killed for the Name of Christ, but he that will endure to the end, the same shall be saved. Many Christian hearts shall grow cold because of the abundance of lawlessness that will fill the earth. They will be offended and fall away, but God's protection policy guarantees that those who dwell in that Secret Place, under His authority, shall overcome spiritually, ethically and morally even if it is at the point of laying down your life

In the last days, the antichrist will come on the political scene and will persecute the saints of the Most High God, setting up himself to be God, and will give his mark: 666, to those who will worship him, with economic benefits (Rev. 13:16-18). Those who do not receive his mark will not be able to buy or sell. There will be trying times for the people of God.

The beast or antichrist will make war with the saints and overcome them (Rev. 13:7). How does he overcome them? Verse 15 records:

"...as many as would not worship the image of the beast should be killed."

He overcame the saints in a physical sense by killing them. Jesus admonishes us not to fear those who are able to kill the body but are not able to kill the soul (Matt. 10:28) They may overcome you physically but by holding fast to the truth even unto death, you overcome them spiritually, ethically and morally for they unable to destroy the soul. Those who shall be killed in the book of revelation are described:

"And I saw as it were a sea of glass mingled with fire: and them that had gotten the victory over the beast, and over his image, and over his mark, and over the number of his name, stand on the sea of glass, having the harps of God" (Rev. 15:2).

These are victors, overcomers, and more than conquerors who were challenged to receive the mark of the beast but refused and were consequently killed. God's saints boldly overcame Satan's accusations and onslaught by the blood of the Lamb and the word of their testimony and did not love their lives even unto death (Rev. 12:11).

God's protection policy provides for spiritual preservation for those who will persevere unto the end. Now it is time to seek the Lord like never before and prepare yourself against the things that are coming on the earth so that you will be able to stand and be saved in the end. I encourage you to appropriate the biblical principles written in this book and live under God's protection.

Bibliography

Edersheim, A. (1995) "Bible History: Old Testament." Massachusetts: Hendrickson Publishers, Inc.

Laid Harris, R. et al. (1980) "Theological Wordbook of the Old Testament," Vol. 1&2. Chicago: Moody Press.

Oyakhilome, C. (2000) "How to Make Your Faith Work." Lagos: Love World Publications

Vine, W. E. (1985) "An Expository Dictionary of New Testament Words." Chicago: Moody Press.

www.ingramcontent.com/pod-product-compliance
Lightning Source LLC
Chambersburg PA
CBHW021129300426
44113CB00006B/351